THE POTENTIAL

Like no other functional area, operations is well-stocked with promising tools and techniques. To name a few:

> Just-in-time inventory, participative management, statistical process control, automation, streamlining, joint ventures, computerization, materials requirements planning, quality circles, preventive and predictive maintenance, scheduling systems, total employee involvement, focus groups.... The list goes on and on.

THE PROBLEM

Successful implementation requires change. And change gives rise to employee resistance. It's universal: Work forces cling to the status quo. Too many technically promising programs have been undermined as a result.

THE SOLUTION

Managers must deal directly with the nontechnical issue of change management. They must develop and implement a plan for creating and controlling change. So many potential benefits hang in the balance, nothing should be left to chance.

THIS BOOK IS YOUR KEY TO SOLVING THE PROBLEM AND ACHIEVING FULL POTENTIAL.

MANAGING CHANGE IN THE 1990s

MANAGING CHANGE IN THE 1990s

STRATEGIES FOR THE OPERATIONS MANAGER

Tom Terez

ARROW ASSOCIATES
Charlotte, North Carolina

MANAGING CHANGE IN THE 1990s:
STRATEGIES FOR THE OPERATIONS MANAGER

Arrow Associates, P.O. Box 470869, Charlotte, North Carolina 28247

Library of Congress Card Number: 90-81583
ISBN 0-9626463-0-X
First printing 1990, second printing 1991

TO THE READER

When *Managing Change in the 1990s* was first published in August 1990, it quickly became clear that change-management issues are a big source of concern in Corporate America. The first print-run sold out in record time. This book is part of the second printing.

Managers who bought up that first print-run come from a wide cross-section of companies. Included are Owens-Corning, Miller Brewing, U.S. Postal Service, Caterpillar, Deere & Co., Parker Hannifin, Westinghouse, Southern Bell, Continental Bank, Avacelle, Boeing, and many others. Sales have been evenly divided between manufacturing and service companies.

I've received notes and calls from some of the book buyers. All of them face unique change-management challenges. They've turned to *Managing Change in the 1990s* for help in planning and implementing their improvement efforts.

I'd like to hear from you, too, as you create and control change. Drop me a line, and while you're at it, include any comments you may have regarding this book. Direct letters to Arrow Associates, P.O. Box 470869, Charlotte NC 28247.

I look forward to hearing from you.

Tom Terez

CONTENTS

INTRODUCTION

"We're our own worst enemy. Our levels of work-in-process and finished goods inventories are way too high. We need to seize control once and for all. Find a solution and I'll back you all the way, whatever it takes."

The production manager of Starmark Manufacturing Co. had heard these words before. Most of the words, that is. "Find a solution and I'll back you all the way, whatever it takes." That comment was a first. About time, the production manager mused.

For too many years, Starmark had been plagued by excessive inventories and unpredictable delivery delays. The lack of control translated into a staggering annual expense, and two prized customers had taken their orders elsewhere. The president, meanwhile, balked time and again when asked to support full-scale solutions to Starmark's problems. Years passed, and the situation grew worse. Now, finally, the production manager had been handed his long-awaited mandate. He could bring to the company what it desperately needed: major change in the operations department.

During the last several years, the production manager had carried around certain convictions. He had a system in mind—a system that could put an end to Starmark's problems and, in the long term, boost its market position. The manager had worked with the system at another company, where he witnessed significant benefits: reduced setup times, reduced work-in-process inventory, faster delivery. The industry called it just-in-time (JIT) inventory.

The production manager considered it Starmark's last and best hope for pulling production out of its costly rut.

Enthused by JIT's obvious potential, the manager single-handedly devised an implementation plan. He made the calculations, developed the system, drafted the documentation, and secured the necessary equipment. Then he pitched the entire concept to his fellow operations employees as a first step to implementation. They listened, and they nodded politely. But when it came time to turn the plan into action, support was nowhere to be found. Some people didn't know exactly what to do. Others knew what to do but preferred not to do it. As far as they were concerned, the plant had been doing just fine without JIT. Why add confusion? The operations manager stated his case a second time, and again, his fellow employees nodded politely. But again, apparent agreement did not mean total acceptance. Far from it.

Two years after officially launching the JIT program, the operations manager is still struggling to make it a full-fledged part of the operation. Inventory control remains elusive, and other departments continue to point fingers at operations, holding it accountable for Starmark's earnings slump. The manager now privately contends it would have been better to fine-tune the old system rather than attempt a major change. Echoing his fellow employees, he asks: Why add confusion?

Stories like this one unfold each working day at operations the world over. The change process may be mostly technical (as in the case of Starmark) or cultural, or somewhere in between. Nearly every operations employee has played a real-life role in some type of internal change. Most have experienced the frustration and fear that change invariably brings. Many regard change warily; it is something to be treated, and accepted, cautiously.

Veteran managers know internal change as a powerful force that can propel an operation to significant improvements. The force is difficult to start, however, and difficult to control once it has been started. Facing resistance to change, some managers throw up their hands and allow the organization to return to the days and ways of the past. For nearly all managers, directing change tops the list of managerial challenges.

This book provides guidance. It outlines a practical approach for managing technical and cultural change in operations—the functional area responsible for generating output. The recommendations you read in the following pages can be put to work in any operations-related change effort. They make change easier to initiate and easier to control.

The book is divided into three parts. Part I lays a broad foundation for managing change. Operations and change are highlighted, with examples that put a real-life spin on the text. Part II consists of three in-depth case studies detailing major change efforts at Cleveland Electric Illuminating Co., Nucor Corp., and Reynolds Metals Co. These accounts give you an insider's view of change management in action. You will learn about strategies and techniques, personalities and problems. You will see what management did right and what it did wrong. You will be able to play armchair manager, putting yourself in management's position and making your own decisions on the basis of detailed case information.

In Part III, all the preceding material is refined to leave you with the most valuable nuggets of practical information. Chapter 6 identifies five change-management issues and five related strategies. These form the basis of an agenda of detailed tactics you can draw from when forming a change-management plan. Keep in mind this simple flow:

Operations Issue ⇒ Change-Management Strategy ⇒ Series of Change-Management Tactics

The tactics, presented in full at the end of Chapter 6, are thorough and practical. They are the tools you will use to bring about change and make it stick. Precise directions on how to use them are given in Chapter 7, which explains the four steps in drafting an action plan for launching and leading change.

At this stage, you may want to preview the issues and strategies, and even to flip through the agenda of tactics. This will provide you with a useful frame of reference for thinking about the case studies. For a list of issues and strategies, turn to Chapter 6. Tactics are presented at the end of the chapter.

PART I

Chapter 1 turns the spotlight on change management and the operations function. The case is made that both are essential if individual companies, and Corporate America as a whole, are to survive in the short term and thrive in the coming century. The chapter then presents several examples. Each real-life story illustrates some facet of change in the operations environment. Together, the examples underscore the need for a practical method for managing change.

The groundwork is completed in Chapter 2, which explains the idea that successful change efforts typically unfold in three distinct stages. The chapter examines each stage, forming a change-management framework. The concepts are then brought to life by a return trip to Starmark Manufacturing. The three-stage process comes up again in Chapter 7, where it's worked into the action plan for managing change.

1

MANAGING CHANGE: AN OPERATIONS NECESSITY

Managers have an arsenal of techniques and technologies capable of improving an operation. Just-in-time inventory, mentioned in the Starmark story, is just one example. Consider these other operations tools: materials requirements planning (MRP), statistical process control (SPC), quality circles, forecasting, computer simulation, computer-aided design, computer-aided manufacturing. The list goes on and on.

Properly used, these tools can work wonders. But implementation requires change, and change must be managed. It's not enough to send employees a memo informing them that a new technique will replace an old technique "effective immediately." Nor is it sufficient simply to install new technology, expecting employees to adopt it because it is there. Change must be implemented in an organized and controlled way, and for this, managers require a systematic change-management method. Properly developed, such a method is a tool in the same way that JIT, MRP, and SPC are tools.

In many operations departments, unfortunately, managers suffer from technical myopia. Much of their time is spent dealing with well-defined technical issues, like statistics showing trends in equipment uptime or reports summarizing labor utilization and productivity. Educational backgrounds tend to be in technical areas like engineering, physics, and mathematics. For many operations managers, change represents something of a gray area. Their education does not prepare them for it. There are no clearly defined change-management rules or easy-to-use formulas. Nor are there any guarantees—either that managing change will assure its success or that neglecting it will doom the change right from the start. Faced with all this, operations managers often restrict their vision to management duties that match their expertise and make them most comfortable. They ignore important change issues, giving resistance to change plenty of room to take root. All too often, the end result is a failed change effort.

General Motors provides an example. In the early 1970s, the company built a plant in Lordstown, Ohio, that promised to be on the leading edge of manufacturing. Designed for production of the Chevrolet Vega, the plant was equipped with the most advanced auto-making technology available at the time, and managers believed this would translate into record-high productivity. What GM neglected, however, were the many cultural factors involved in the change. Workers felt that the plant's technological sophistication removed much of the challenge from their jobs. Pride became an issue, fueling resistance to the new production process. Complaints also emerged that management was speeding up the production line. As absenteeism grew, quality and productivity fell. Eventually, resistance gave way to a wildcat strike.[1]

Today, few critics would fault the plant's technical design. Explaining where things went wrong takes most observers to the technical myopia that afflicted management. Preoccupied with the technical aspects of the new plant, they neglected the cultural components of the change. In addition, they ignored the need to *manage* change; they simply provided new equipment and expected change to occur automatically. Since the plant was new, managers may not have viewed the installation of new equipment as a complicated change issue. Yet Lordstown workers were familiar with many other, older automobile plants, and they used these as benchmarks. The older plants were the norm, and anything else represented change. If GM's operations managers had broadened their definition of the Lordstown change to include cultural elements, and used this definition as a foundation in building a change-management plan, the Lordstown plant would have come much closer to meeting GM's high expectations.

Both a cause and effect of technical myopia can be found in operations literature. Operations textbooks and journals focus almost exclusively on technical areas. The material is densely scientific. The nontechnical area of change management is seldom mentioned. Rarer still is any mention of the cultural features of operations environments.

Articles in the popular business press tell of changes in operations, but they seldom include analysis of the change-management process. Description of the change typically receives one or two paragraphs of coverage. Reporters seem more interested in events leading up to the change and the impact on the organization as a whole.

Take, for example, a *Wall Street Journal* article titled, "GM to Retool Pittsburgh Stamping Plant to Parts Factory, Avoiding Close-down." The article, which is 11 paragraphs long, includes only three sentences on management of the change process: "The new work for the plant has been made possible in part by the local union's willingness to make cost-saving changes to work rules.... The plant's new business will be phased in over the next few years. Union officials said the size of Pittsburgh's work force will shrink from its current level of 1,400, but added that cuts will take place through attrition, not layoffs."[2] In all fairness, it's not the *Journal*'s responsibility, with this story and most others, to provide detailed information on *how* change is managed. The point is, operations managers who make the *Journal* their main source of information are unlikely to pick up insights into directing change.

Another layer of literature includes the many articles on organizational change found in periodicals like the *Journal of Business Strategy*, *Organizational Dynamics*, *California Management Review*, and the *Strategic Management Journal*. Most of these articles provide excellent theoretical insights into the change process and ways to manage it. But few articles deal specifically with change management in the operations environment. What's more, most articles examine only cultural change, as opposed to technical change. Yet, change in operations often has a technical slant. Academic articles can be excessively theoretical; concepts are not practical enough to be of much use to the operations manager.

As you can see, this book fills a void. It describes a practical method for managing change in the operations environment, supplying a tool that operations managers need to implement change successfully. The tool is essential. It complements techniques and technologies already available to operations managers.

BUSINESS BASICS

Skeptics may question the wisdom of narrowing the book's focus to *operations*-related change. But this focus makes perfect sense when we take stock of the past, present, and future of American business. Operations has real bottom-line impact on our manufacturing and service industries. Practically every business depends on it; a failure in operations has significant consequences for customers and for the company as a whole. The pages of business history are filled with examples showing just how powerful operations can be in boosting or busting a company's best intentions.

Consider two well-publicized airline mergers: Republic and Northwest in 1986, USAir and Piedmont in 1989. Imagine having to combine computer systems, baggage-handling efforts, operational facilities, ground operations, and more. Throw in thousands of employees, millions of demanding consumers, tough competition, and a couple holiday seasons. The result, to no one's surprise, was a massive change-management challenge. And both mergers ran into some heavy turbulence. Critics—ranging from objective reporters to irate passengers—made clear their collective belief that things could have been managed much better.

It's difficult to gauge how a slip in on-time averages and an increase in consumer complaints affected the bottom line. But in today's no-holds-barred airline industry, in which on-time averages are routinely posted in daily newspapers, passengers can be less than forgiving. A change-management plan that leaves nothing to chance is essential for pulling together what is often a conflicting set of technical and cultural forces.

Manufacturing also provides many examples of the make-or-break role operations plays in the success of the organization. Consider Caterpillar Inc., where a full-scale effort is underway to modernize nearly all the company's 30 plants worldwide. The "Plant with a Future" program, as it's billed, aims to cut expenses, improve quality, and speed up delivery times. The company has outlined four broad strategies: consolidate, automate, simplify, and integrate. At the core of the effort are two nuts-and-bolts operations strategies: automation and just-in-time inventory.[3] Other key elements include flexible manufacturing, materials requirements planning, tool standardization, and automated materials handling. The company obviously has identified operations as the functional area best suited for restoring the company's competitive strength.

Caterpillar's actions contrast the collective behavior that typified American business during the 1980s. This was the "dollar-sign decade," when business seemed mesmerized by finance and investment banking, when paper-shuffling and short-term thinking were seen as the best ways to make money. The trend was obvious among graduate business students, who flocked to Wall Street in search of quick fortune. The media also climbed aboard, cranking out story after story about leveraged buy-outs, takeovers, greenmail, mergers, divestments. Operations became a mere footnote as investment bankers came to dominate Corporate America.

Then, suddenly, the country woke up to a costly day called Black Monday. Wall Street's hypnotic effect diminished considerably, along with the number of job opportunities. The stock market rebounded during the next few years, but the paper-shuffling trend seemed to be approaching a point of exhaustion. The collapse finally came in February 1990, when Corporate America was rocked by the fall of Drexel Burnham Lambert. Drexel had been the undisputed champ of Wall Street, ruling the buy-out business with a powerful weapon called the junk bond. The firm's Chapter 11 demise made clear that the heady investment-banking days had come to an irrevocable end.

The Drexel saga is the biggest—but certainly not the only—piece of evidence of dramatic change. All across Corporate America, companies have moved away from the 1980s way of making money. Like Caterpillar, they are striving to achieve competitive strength by improving the functional area directly responsible for producing goods and services. There's talk again of productivity, efficiency, and other nuts-and-bolts concepts as operations regains corporate respect. In board room after board room, it's back to basics.

Case in point: General Electric Co. During most of the 1980s, GE Chairman John F. Welch Jr. seemed intent on growth through acquisition. Now, the goal is to make the most of what's already in hand. Acquisition has become a part of the old vocabulary; the new catch-word is productivity. Accordingly, GE has turned to its factory floors for ways to make manufacturing more profitable. Streamlining, teamwork, and product redesign are just several of the major changes that have emerged. Much more will happen in the 1990s. Welch has appointed GE's first productivity czar and outlined an ambitious goal for the new decade: annual productivity increases of 5%. The effort is off to a running start. Net income for 1989 was up about 16% from the previous year, due in large part to increases in productivity.[4]

For America's manufacturing and service companies, a return to basics appears to be a competitive necessity. Just look at the trade figures for manufactured goods, which are always a good economic barometer. From 1980 through 1986, the dollar value of U.S. exports remained flat while imports shot up more than 200%. "Made in the U.S.A." exports accounted for 54% of the country's total import-export pie in 1980. By 1986, the slice had dwindled to 35%.[5] Exports finally are starting to show signs of life as we head into the 1990s, but the devastation is clear. The manufacturing sector will have to work hard and smart in order to rebuild America's export strength.

The service industry, which accounts for about 71% of total U.S. output, faces the same troubles. As overseas competitors improve their service output, America's lead shrinks. Analysts often point to productivity as the culprit. They speak the truth, since the country's annual rate of productivity growth in services has declined steadily since the 1940s.

But peel back the layers and you'll find more fundamental problems, most of which relate to operations. It turns out that many American service companies are at a productivity disadvantage because they cannot effectively integrate computers into the work place.[6] Managers have come to realize that successful integration requires much more than installation and a good instruction manual.

Some operations veterans like to associate their functional area exclusively with manufacturing. This may have been appropriate back in the days when manufactured goods made up the bulk of U.S. output, but no longer. Consider these labor statistics: From 1980 through 1988, the number of employees in manufacturing jobs slipped 4%. Meanwhile, in the service industry, employee ranks grew 96%.[7]

Like it or not, America is putting an increasing number of its economic eggs in the service basket. The success of this sector—not to mention its survival—will depend in large part on how well the operations function is managed.

STORIES FROM THE OPERATIONS FRONT

The best way to introduce change management in the operations environment is to provide an inventory of examples. Real-life stories reveal challenges posed by technical and cultural change. They also show the subtle and not-so-subtle differences that characterize major change efforts, confirming the common notion that no two change processes are identical.

First, consider the banking industry, in which internal change has been prompted by external change. Rapid advances in electronic technology have changed the rules of the banking game, adding a potentially powerful competitive weapon to the industry. Managers have been handed two options: adopt the new technology, or try to compete with antiquated weapons. Most banks have opted for the high-tech approach. Yet many are discovering that the promise of state-of-the-art technology can look far out of reach during the implementation stage. That's when things get bogged down—when the equipment is integrated into the operation.

During the past two decades, the banking industry's collective experience has become a classic study in change management. Operations employees have had to learn how to work with new forms of technology. Offices have been reorganized in terms of personnel and office structure to accommodate the technical changes. In some cases, entirely new positions have been created. The implications are enormous and continue to evolve. The common thread is change.

In the late 1960s, Citibank's "back office," the area that handles many of the bank's operations functions, began experiencing significant performance problems. Under the direction of Citibank's Operating Group, the back office had become a bastion of predictability. Many employees originally hired to work in the department went on to spend their entire careers there. Needless to say, the environment was not ripe for change. But the pace of industry change, especially in terms of technology, only quickened. Customers began expecting higher levels of service—levels that Citibank found increasingly difficult to provide. The bank had to take action.

John Reed, then head of the Operating Group, led the charge. He began by hiring several operations executives from Ford Motor Co. His thinking: The Ford managers could reorient the bank's operations department to resemble a factory's production system.

The changes that followed affected nearly every facet of the back-office operation, from technical issues like computer equipment to cultural issues like attitudes toward work. The change stirred controversy and complaints. In fact, the Citibank saga has become a well-known case study, prompting debates at business schools on right and wrong ways to manage change. Undisputed, however, are the impressive results for the bank and at least some of the people involved in the change. The department became a big money-maker, and Reed became the bank's chairman.[8]

Citibank had little choice in deciding to change. With significant changes afoot in the industry, the effort to alter operations became a matter of corporate survival. The method of managing the change at Citibank, however, could have been handled differently. Computer equipment literally arrived overnight with little advance notice from management. Most employees working under the Operating Group arrived on Monday morning to find terminals sitting on their desks. Considering that employees were so unfamiliar with change, it's no surprise the move sparked anger and resentment. This was aggravated by the fact that the change process was managed almost exclusively by outsiders brought in by Reed.

The insurance industry is experiencing a similar situation: Computer technology offers tremendous competitive potential, yet operations are finding it difficult to integrate the technology into the work place. Many firms have tried, but few have fully achieved the strides in productivity that computers could make possible. The central issue involves managing the change: Unless managers find a way to manage change effectively, technology-related productivity gains will remain elusive. What makes all this so serious is that U.S. insurance companies annually spend some $7 billion on computer hardware.[9]

The parcel shipping industry offers another interesting look at the importance of change management. During the past several years, United Parcel Service has worked to integrate technological advances into its operation. The effort is being driven in large part by competitive forces; Federal Express has turned its technical savvy into a competitive advantage, and UPS must respond. Because UPS has built its strong market position while sticking to some decades-old operations techniques, the use of high-tech equipment means a rather significant change.

"Big Brown" launched its technical foray by acquiring two small computer firms: one to provide software, the other to design and produce hardware. Next came field tests involving a fleet of 35 UPS messenger cars in Los Angeles. The objective: to try out everything from electronic vehicle tracking to computerized route directions. Separately, the company installed electronic scanners in some of its sorting centers. The advanced equipment quickens package flow and allows for precise tracking of individual parcels.[10]

The march of high technology continues at UPS, moving ahead at a steady, manageable pace. By the end of 1991, the company will have spent about $1.4 billion over five years to set up a state-of-the-art computer operation. (Quite a contrast to 1985, when the company's total computer-systems expense, including salaries, was $20 million.) The objective, according to one executive, is to "have the technology in place to transform UPS into a totally different operation."[11] It seems like a gross understatement to say change is underway.

While the steady approach is working for UPS, at General Motors, things have tended to bog down. GM has struggled to increase productivity at its plants through automation, flexible production methods, and other approaches. Although many of these strategies have succeeded at other companies, GM's efforts have been hampered by union anxiety. The union wants guarantees that change will not jeopardize job security.[12]

During fall 1987, GM and the United Autoworkers worked together to create a mutually acceptable game plan. Among the features was an opportunity for union members to make their own recommendations for boosting efficiency and reducing the amount of contract work. Most observers thought things were moving along quickly. Then, with implementation, the process began to slow. As one union member put it, "You're not going to sprinkle some magic powder in six months and fix 80 years' worth of problems."[13]

The situation has evolved since the discussions in 1987. But the problem remains the same—not only for GM, but also for other auto makers that want to improve productivity by injecting new techniques into the operations environment. Employees have made job security a rallying point for resisting change. Meanwhile, management is beginning to realize the complexities involved in moving new operations ideas from the drawing board to the factory floor. Having felt the pressure of resistance to change, they are seeking a methodical approach for managing change in the operations environment.

Joint ventures are another area in which change is a constant. When companies first team up to pursue common objectives, each tends to cling to a unique set of operating methods and cultural traits. But over time, the players must compromise. They discover that a common objective simply isn't enough to foster a successful working relationship. Organizations must change in ways that bring them closer together. Each must make slight technical and cultural changes to strengthen the link to the other company. If companies reject this—if they pursue a shared goal while ignoring the technical and cultural conflicts—they jeopardize the entire joint venture.

This harsh fact is becoming increasingly apparent to American managers involved in joint ventures with Japanese firms. In many cases, technical and cultural styles are completely different, if not altogether contradictory. Some joint-venture veterans point to those differences—and the managerial inability to neutralize them—as one reason for many joint-venture failures. Additional forces are at work, of course, but it's clear that operations managers must deal with change when entering a joint-venture situation. Success depends in large part on how well that change is managed.

2

CHANGE IN THREE ACTS

Before plunging into the nitty-gritty detail of actual change efforts, it's useful to step back and develop a macro understanding of how change can be successfully managed. An overview reduces for managers the risk of drowning in detail. When all seems lost, they can grab hold of the comforting simplicity of an overview. Veteran change managers may not need the warning, but all others, pay heed: Your change-management efforts will be buffeted by all sorts of complications. Prepare yourself by mastering the basics.

If you think this macro look involves theory, well, you're correct. But most of the following material is theoretical in the same way that basic laws of physics are theoretical: They remain theories, like the theory of gravity, yet they are seldom if ever disputed. No worthy physicist would feel safe without understanding something as basic as gravity. Similarly, no manager should feel secure without a thorough knowledge of basic change theory.

LEWIN'S LEGACY: UNFREEZE, MOVE, REFREEZE

Social scientist Kurt Lewin defined change as a three-stage process: unfreeze, move, and refreeze. Remember these three steps. They are essential components of any successful change-management effort.

Because Lewin published his studies in the 1950s, some critics say the concepts are a bit too dusty for modern-day organizations.

What's surprising, however, is how well Lewin's results have withstood the test of time. Successful change-management efforts at leading-edge companies still fit remarkably well into Lewin's three-step framework. Managers who address all three steps—knowingly, we hope, or even unknowingly—invariably succeed in their effort to manage internal change. On the other hand, managers who skip one or two steps typically find the change to be short-lived, if change occurs at all.

STEP #1: UNFREEZE

When employees have been doing things a certain way for many years, they feel secure. They become experts at their jobs. They know where to find the paper clips, where to find replacement drive chains, where to turn when inventory falls below a preset minimum. They know when to call the production supervisor, when to take a break, when to go that extra mile for a customer. They become locked—frozen—into a certain way of doing things.

How does change appear to these people? Not very good, to say the least. Put yourself in the shoes of someone who has been working competently for five years in a production role at a major plant. Contemplate the questions you would ask if you were called on to change the way you carried out your job: Why should I trade my complete understanding of my job for a situation filled with so much uncertainty? Why should I take on the additional risk that goes with change? Why should this happen to me when I have performed competently all along? After so many years, why does this happen now? All are reasonable questions, and you can bet they'll be asked. Management must provide good answers if the change process is to proceed.

These questions point up the need for motivation. Personnel must be given a reason for going along with the change process. This is the only way to unfreeze the work force. If the reasons are not persuasive—less persuasive, that is, than the reasons for remaining "frozen"—management will not succeed at implementing lasting change. Motivation is the key component of the "unfreezing" stage.

Fortunately, managers have access to a variety of motivational tools. Money is only the most obvious. Consider a company that wants to install a new computer system for managing inventory.

Workers are told the system will require major changes in the way they perform their jobs. To compensate for this, however, a bonus that reflects decreases in inventory holding costs will be given to each worker. If the workers decide the potential bonus overrides the discomfort of changing their job routine, management is off to an excellent start in securing the change.

Motivation doesn't have to involve dollars. Management may try to unfreeze the work force by showing that change will create a more hospitable or enjoyable work environment. This vision of a "better future" must be presented in very specific terms if it's to carry any persuasive weight. "Better" may mean that in two years, the company will be ahead of its primary competitor in market share, assuring job security for at least the next five years. Or "better" may mean improved working conditions: a new lounge area, significant reductions in the danger involved in high-risk jobs, an additional 15-minute break each day. There are many possibilities.

Another form of motivation is problem recognition. Workers are more likely to accept change if they feel that the current operating method is inferior or ineffective. For instance, management may inform all personnel that unless a change is implemented within six months, the company's competitive position will deteriorate, perhaps to the point where the company will have to lay off workers. A company may couple this kind of talk with dramatic action—for instance, transferring production of one product line to an overseas location to show concern about expenses.

Such moves can make a strong impression on employees. But managers sometimes take things too far, creating an adversarial situation that takes years to overcome. Remember the objective: to motivate employees to accept change by convincing them that change is absolutely necessary. By pointing out problems, managers can make a strong case for change. Turning problems into pointed threats, on the other hand, can lay the foundation for a solid wall of employee resistance.

STEP #2: MOVE

Once the organization has been "unfrozen," it's time for the "movement" step. This is the stage most commonly associated with change, since it involves the actual transition to new operating methods. It's when the most visible aspects of the change process emerge.

Management must move quickly from the unfreezing step to the movement step. Any delay suggests a lack of management commitment, and nothing can more seriously undermine tentative worker support for the change. To speed up the transition between steps, and to make the transition very visible and direct, managers can employ a so-called kill event. This involves some distinct and public display that the old operating method has been pushed into the past—that it's time to forge ahead with the new operating method. The kill event offers indisputable proof to all employees that the change is for real, marking the final and complete break with the past.

To get the most out of this transition technique, managers should try to involve workers who will be affected by the change. In an office setting, for instance, workers may spend an entire day shifting office equipment to prepare for the next-day installation of a computer network. This will involve them in the change process itself. Compare this to having employees arrive the next morning to face an entirely new office layout complete with the invading computers terminals.

Following the kill event, it's time to move on to full implementation. This is when the change manager must turn into a master juggler who can deal with several important issues at once. For one, management must provide ample opportunity for workers to adopt the new operating methods. If the company has just installed a computer system, for instance, management should see to it that appropriate personnel have sufficient access to computer terminals. Workers must be able to try out the changes. This becomes vital if some employees remain doubtful the change will last. Their likely question: "If management has not committed enough resources, should I commit myself to the change? Perhaps this isn't what management really wants." By providing adequate resources up front, managers head off employee doubts while fostering employee commitment.

Training is another key component of the movement step. Employees cannot be expected simply to pick up the new methods on their own. There are no two ways about it: Employees must be taught how to perform all functions made necessary by the change. Training will be looked upon as a resource. If management provides less instruction than is necessary, employees will begin to doubt management's commitment.

Throughout the movement stage, employee participation is a critical variable. People want to have, or at least perceive that they have, control over their professional destinies. Researchers have drawn up a long list of ways to build a participatory environment. Some critics warn against excessive participation, noting it can soak up precious work time and yield few constructive results. Finding the right balance is among the many decisions that managers must make while managing change.

Managerial commitment, which already has been mentioned, cannot be emphasized enough. Without a clear and public display of support for the new way of doing things, management will capsize its own efforts. Everyone who is affected by the change will be looking to management for its attitude toward the change. It isn't enough for management to say: "Well, since these changes are being made, that is sufficient evidence that management wants them." This is one case in which a simple assumption can have terrible consequences.

Management must take a front and center position, showing support for all efforts to adopt the changes. A single memo to workers usually will not suffice. A weekly memo updating results certainly is better, but also may be too passive to have any measurable impact. Routine walk-throughs by top managers, on the other hand, will show active interest in and concern for the change process. It will make clear to all workers where management truly stands on the change issue.

During the movement step, workers typically respond in two ways. In the first phase, they test the new operating methods. They may remain skeptical, but they have been motivated to keep an open mind and explore. To move into the second phase, motivation must be sufficiently strong, and a "kill event" needs to take place. There must be ample training, if needed, and obvious commitment from top management. Then, workers can move into the second phase, during which they accept the new operating method as their own. The change thus becomes the new and accepted rule for carrying out the daily job routine. Management's new method unconditionally becomes the workers' new method.

The concise description above belies the complexity of the change process. A lot can go wrong during the movement step—and before it. If one or two key workers remain unfrozen, for example, they can threaten the entire change. During the movement itself, problems can affect any of the key components: the kill event, training, employee participation, management commitment, acceptance of the new operating methods. Just one weak spot—insufficient training, for instance—can hobble an entire change effort.

The juggler metaphor seems a bit trivial, but it conveys not only the hectic nature of the manager's job, but also the diligence required to ensure that none of the balls is dropped. After all, the juggler, like the change manager, wants the act to be a rousing success.

STEP #3: REFREEZE

If the first two steps are properly managed, the time will come when employees accept the new methods. At this point, management needs to "refreeze" the work force. This ensures that employees will not revert to their old, familiar operating methods.

It's tempting to think the refreezing stage is easy. If you have successfully led the work force through the change process, your confidence level is likely to be high, and for good reason. But operations-related changes, like any type of organizational change, consist of constant movement. And movement is difficult to control regardless of the form it takes. It's all a matter of inertia: Will you be able to stop the movement right where you want it? If you can, for how long? There's also an assessment problem: Precisely where are the collective attitudes, work habits, and knowledge at the point of full implementation? How will you know when you have reached the ideal point?

For instance, do workers sufficiently understand the new computerized baggage-handling system, or is additional training required? Do the handlers fully accept the new system, or do they still question the extent of management's commitment? The old way of doing things still lurks in the minds of all employees. If the "unfreeze" and "move" stages have not been completely successful, employees may find it easier simply to revert to their traditional work habits. Does this seem to be happening?

Unless questions like these can be answered with reasonable certainty, deciding when to refreeze will be a risky undertaking.

Again, managerial discretion is required. The manager who keeps close to the work force, and who manages the change with care, will be better able to make these requisite judgment calls. As for understanding what's involved in the refreezing step, consider two activities: reinforcement and support. Both are essential to the refreezing step, and they must be aggressively pursued to ensure success.

With reinforcement, management shows its approval with the current work. This can involve keeping workers up to date on the ongoing results of new methods and techniques. For instance, the managers of a printing company may post weekly data that show productivity increases resulting from new printing equipment. This can fill in the picture of the "better future" that management talked about during the unfreeze step. Reinforcement also can be achieved through compensation. Bonuses are a very tangible way for management to show its approval. Training is another form of reinforcement. In some cases, workers will require several rounds of training, especially if the change involves complicated equipment or significantly different operating methods. Ongoing training not only helps workers, but also shows management's commitment to the change.

Support is slightly different. Workers will have questions about their new jobs, and management will need to make itself available to answer them. For instance, if a worker comes forward and explains that he or she simply doesn't feel competent using a certain computer system, the manager should be prepared to provide a solution. Sending that person back into the system without giving proper support will assure a much more serious problem somewhere down the line.

Consider another example: A worker approaches her manager and complains she cannot get enough computer time. The worker's job requires about four hours of computer access daily, yet a terminal is free on average only two hours. If the manager, after determining that four hours is a reasonable amount of time, balks at supporting the worker, management has sent out a confusing signal. As these signals build up, workers will question management's commitment to the change and may contemplate returning to their old operating methods. On the other hand, if the manager solves the problem (perhaps by securing an additional computer, or shifting around work times), the worker directly involved in the situation will know definitively that the new operating method has management's full commitment. The worker remains committed to the change. What's more, the incident is likely to send a signal to other workers that tangible support for the change does exist.

Managerial vigilance is vital during the refreezing step, and it remains important long after the work force has fully accepted the new methods. All organizations are in a constant state of drift, and managers must protect the results of their successful change efforts.

Turnover is one force contributing to organizational drift. Consider a company in which operations managers have spent several years reshaping the culture. Suddenly, the company changes its policy of hiring strictly from within and opens its doors to outsiders. Will the new culture, representing several years of hard change-management work, be threatened? Management must decide how the new hiring policy will stir the ongoing, underlying current of change. Will it push the work force away from the optimal position at which it was frozen? If so, reinforcement may be necessary. The required judgment call will be considerably less risky if management remains fully aware of the dynamic nature of the organization.

THE STARMARK STORY REVISITED

Remember the story of Starmark Manufacturing described in the introduction? At last report, the production manager seemed ready to give up on a newly installed just-in-time inventory system. Employees, it seemed, could not be made to change. They wanted to stick with their old procedures no matter what JIT could offer.

Let's revisit Starmark and rewrite the story. For this second version, imagine that the production manager is well-versed in the concept of the three change steps: unfreeze, move, and refreeze. We start from the beginning....

"We're our own worst enemy. Our levels of work-in-process and finished goods inventories are way too high. We need to seize control once and for all. Find a solution and I'll back you all the way, whatever it takes."

The production manager of Starmark Manufacturing Co. had heard these words before. Most of the words, that is. "Find a solution and I'll back you all the way, whatever it takes." That comment was a first. About time, the production manager mused.

For too many years, Starmark had been plagued by excessive inventories and unpredictable delivery delays. The lack of control translated into a staggering annual expense, and two prized customers had taken their orders elsewhere. The president, meanwhile, balked time and again when asked to support full-scale solutions to Starmark's problems. Years passed, and the situation grew worse. Now, finally, the production manager had been handed his long-awaited mandate. He could bring to the company what it desperately needed: major change in the operations department.

During the last several years, the production manager had carried around certain convictions. He had a system in mind—a system that would put an end to Starmark's problems and, in the long term, boost its market position. The manager had worked with the system at another company, where he witnessed significant benefits: reduced setup times, reduced work-in-process inventory, faster delivery. The industry called it just-in-time inventory. The production manager considered it Starmark's last and best hope for pulling production out of its costly rut.

He knew, however, that his enthusiasm alone would not lead to a successful JIT program at Starmark Manufacturing. No, it would be much more complicated. Few of the people whose jobs would be affected by the new system had ever seen JIT in action. They would be dubious, they would be anxious. They would have to be convinced.

As a first step to what he envisioned would be a long journey, the production manager jotted four words on a note pad: motivation, involvement, training, and evaluation. Based on his knowledge of change management, the manager considered these to be the keys to successful JIT implementation. He tore the page from the pad and positioned it in a conspicuous spot on his desk. The page would sit there throughout the next several months as a constant reminder.

Next, the manager made plans to announce the change to all production employees. In preparation, he and his staff gathered thorough industry data showing average work-in-process levels, quality indicators, setup and delivery times, and related inventory measures. The manager arranged the data to show how Starmark stacked up against the competition. The picture wasn't pretty. Compared with companies that had well-run JIT systems, Starmark rated near the bottom. To make matters worse, Starmark encountered those companies each day in the marketplace.

At an introductory meeting, the manager presented this information to key operations managers, along with general information about JIT. The manager emphasized several points:

JIT was a competitive necessity.

It would make lives easier in the long term.

Employees would receive plenty of training.

Employees would be involved in shaping and implementing the program.

The performance evaluation method would change in a way that placed greater importance on teamwork and quality.

During the rest of the day, the manager met with all 90 operations employees in groups of 10 at a time. These meetings covered the same basic points.

Later in the week, each employee received a memo highlighting the competitive basis for the change. The memo noted Starmark's tradition of pride, recalling how employees helped launch a new product line five years earlier that had seized market share from an arch-competitor.

The memo also announced the date of the company-wide JIT kick-off. All production would be halted the following Monday. The company president would begin the day with a few words, after which operations employees would divide into two groups. The day would include a JIT training overview and a question-and-answer session. The next day, production would resume. Individual training, with in-depth instruction for all operations employees, would be held during the following two weeks.

All of this unfolded as planned. Meanwhile, the production manager set up a steering committee to direct the implementation. He chaired this committee. Other members included the vice president for operations, two supervisors, the personnel director, a union representative, the inventory manager, and the production manager's assistant. They met at least twice a week to deal mainly with broad issues related to program installation and change. On an as-needed basis, the committee delegated specific implementation problems to focus groups consisting of additional employees from all levels.

One of these issues dealt with performance evaluation, which the production manager considered a potential sore spot. It no longer made sense for production quantity to be a primary performance indicator. If management measured people against it—especially during the change process—resentment and confusion would start to brew. With the steering committee providing input, a focus group created a new evaluation system that quickly won acceptance among all operations employees.

As JIT became woven into the fabric of the operation, the manager made a point of keeping the reminder sheet on his desk. Motivation, involvement, training, and evaluation. The fabric had flaws. In some places it was not tightly woven. The effort to get people to change would have to continue if the full benefits of JIT were to be realized.

The production manager wondered if he had done enough. There seemed to be something missing, something he had overlooked when leading the JIT charge. He had tapped the department's pride and unity, but that seemed insufficient. Some employees questioned whether the new system was fair. Their contention: that some people ended up working harder than before while others had their lives made easier. Then there was the conflict with upper management over the requirements of JIT. Several managers remained skeptical of the program and its purported benefits. Employees knew this, and an undercurrent of doubt could be felt on the factory floor. Before the new program, things had been so predictable. JIT had shattered this predictability.

The manager leaned over his note pad, as if expecting a solution to write itself. But all he could muster was the word "change"—and a scribbled question mark.

PART II

It's easy to talk in terms of theory. Practice is often very different and considerably more difficult. Mastering the concept of change management is best accomplished through a mix of theory and example. Thus, the following three chapters provide three real-life examples of change in the operations setting. All are straight-as-an-arrow honest and rich in detail. They show the many twists and

EXHIBIT IIA

⇧ Cultural		
	Cultural Change: Nucor Machined Products	Technical and Cultural Change: Alloys Sheet & Plate Plant
		Technical Change: Cleveland Electric Illuminating Co.

Technical ⇨

turns change management can take, enabling us to highlight key concepts and issues that thread through all forms of operations-related change.

The case studies examine major internal changes at Cleveland Electric Illuminating Co., Nucor Corp., and Reynolds Metals Co. Each story is unique in terms of the type of change being managed. Exhibit IIA offers a useful way to distinguish these types.

As you can see, the change at Cleveland Electric Illuminating (CEI) is classified primarily as a technical change; the cultural impact was relatively small. At Nucor, the Fortune 500 steel maker based in Charlotte, N.C., the change had a cultural slant. And at the Alloys Sheet and Plate Plant, a Reynolds Metals facility in Sheffield, Ala., both technical and cultural factors characterized the change process.

The case studies take a departure from most in that they rely heavily on the actual words of the people involved. By letting employees speak for themselves, we get a more accurate sense of their feelings and perceptions regarding change. Analysis is provided throughout each case study, but you are encouraged to "listen" to employees' actual words and draw your own conclusions.

3

PROFILE: TECHNICAL CHANGE AT CLEVELAND ELECTRIC ILLUMINATING CO.

The task seemed simple enough: Approach the property, find the meter, take the readings, enter the readings onto an IBM "mark sense" card. It *was* simple, especially for veteran meter-readers. For 25 years, the job remained unchanged, and meter-reading became one of the constants at Cleveland Electric Illuminating Co.

Then, suddenly, technology made a giant leap forward. Hand-held computers revolutionized the meter-reading task, and companies seized them to gain economic advantage.

CEI managers keenly understood the tremendous potential of computerized meter-reading. They realized that hand-held computers would eliminate the cumbersome card-and-pencil system once and for all, replacing it with a far superior tool for information control. The devices could be used not only to provide meter-readers with additional information, but also to allow for closer monitoring of customers and employees. The data could then be used to determine optimal route structures, guaranteeing significant productivity increases.

No one ever questioned the benefits. What did raise questions, however, was implementation. Management would have to push against the inertia created by 25 years of doing things a certain way. How would the change be accepted?

At the time, CEI had 725,000 residential and commercial customers stretched across northern Ohio. They were serviced by 117 meter-readers, most of whom were very comfortable with their jobs. The entire operation was divided into seven service-center locations. Each was operated autonomously, managed by a field supervisor and manned by a team of meter-readers who began their routes early in the morning and returned to their reporting locations at about 4 p.m. Each field supervisor reported to a service center manager; each of these managers, in turn, reported to one of three district managers.

What risks did the change involve? How would it affect customer service? Did the benefits outweigh the risks? The first two questions could not be answered easily. But management felt it could answer the last question with a definite yes. And so, CEI launched the change in March 1987, opting for a two-phase approach.

In the first phase, meter-readers began using the hand-held computers. The fully programmed devices provided two-way communications: They told meter-readers where to go and what to look for, and the meter-readers responded by entering their readings. At the end of the day, when the readers returned to their service-center locations, the devices were inserted into a computer-linked cradle. Data were automatically transferred to the main system, boosting processing speed, accuracy, and data thoroughness.

John Zelis, a CEI analyst who played a key role in the change process, cited one overriding benefit:

> The ultimate goal with electronic meter-reading (EMR) is that it enabled us, because it has a built-in clock, to watch what was going on in the field locations without having to drive around and follow the meter-readers. In other words, as the day wore on, we could see how fast a meter-reader was reading meters and, most important, at what time he read the meter. So we knew then whether our routing was too short or too long.

The managers let one year pass while data on all routes stacked up in the mainframe. Then, beginning in April 1988, Zelis and three other CEI employees began phase two: readjusting the routes in an attempt to increase productivity. Zelis explained his team's approach:

> At each location, we would target any particular route

> that was being read in six hours or less, and we would say, "That's obviously a short route. We can break the route into several small segments and attach those segments to any other nearby routes that should be increased in size." That's what we did. At the same time, to demonstrate our interest in equity and safety, we decreased the size of routes that simply could not be completed in one day with the reader maintaining a reasonably strong pace.

When CEI entered phase two of the change process, its 725,000 meters were divided into about 1,839 individual routes. The staggering numbers meant considerable work for Zelis' management team. To compound the work load, the company's computer system could not effectively determine the optimal sequence of addresses for each route. It was not enough simply to tell the computer to organize the addresses in sequential order; the most efficient routing system could not be achieved through a strict sequencing of addresses. This very technical part of the job would require a significant measure of human judgment.

Zelis' implementation team came well-equipped for the task. All four members had served as meter-readers, which allowed them to tap a large reserve of personal experience when making judgment calls. The three people working under Zelis' direction included: Jim Warren, a meter-reading supervisor temporarily assigned to the project; Lee Prok, an operations analyst with the company's technical staff; and Steve Strah, who had moved up steadily from meter-reader to person in charge of EMR computer system maintenance.

Like most change efforts, this one faced an external force: namely, a possible utility-rate change. The four-person management team knew all too well that a rate change, coming smack in the middle of a route restructuring, would cause turmoil in many departments. They also knew that a full route restructuring normally required 15 to 18 months to complete. With the rate change expected to take effect in fewer than six months, speed became the order of the day. Results emerged more quickly than the most optimistic observers had predicted.

In June of that year, just two months after the analysis had begun, the management team reached the launch point for partial implementation. The first official use of the new route structures involved meter-readers from two service-center locations. The rest of the centers, five in all, adopted reformulated routes by the end of October. Almost immediately, results began to show up in bottom-line reports. The effort had scaled down the number of routes from 1,839 to 1,600. This amounted to a 13% decrease in the number of routes—a measurement translated as a 13% increase in productivity.

At the time of this writing, with all the difficult change-management work behind them, CEI's managers agreed that the project had succeeded. What's more, employees at all levels said that over the course of the entire change process, as the company evolved from the old system to the new, management steered a very smooth course.

Asked for their observations at the very outset of the change, workers may have given quite different observations. One team member, Steve Strah, recalled a time when things looked considerably less positive.

> We were at the stage where we hadn't laid down the plan to all meter-reading and union personnel. We were basically on a fact-finding tour (at one of our service-center locations). Some readers caught a rumor of what was going on, and a few of them were rather upset—very upset, in fact. At that point, it kind of struck me that if we don't focus our energies on a give-and-take proposition here—working with our employees and not against them—we could have a very large negative impact on those employees. Obviously, we resolved the situation a short time after that. But basically, at that point we said to ourselves, "We could be sitting on a powder keg."

Strah's comments reveal the complexity inherent even in a straightforward technical change. The blueprint for change may look remarkably organized on paper, but turning that blueprint into the real thing can be something else entirely. Yet the CEI management team displayed remarkable skill at the balancing act that change management often becomes. True, technical change is not as vague as cultural change, which makes it comparatively easy to execute. But any change, technical included, can put managers on a tightrope that leaves little room for missteps. The CEI management team combined considerable behind-the-scenes planning with on-the-spot decision-making, as the evolving change process required. The following analysis explores key issues that surfaced during the change.

SHOW AND TELL

Whenever people try to pinpoint the causes of project breakdowns or personnel conflicts, they invariably come up with "a breakdown in communication." This sometimes is the case, but more often, bad communication is a *symptom* of an underlying problem. Mending the relationship requires a process of peeling back layers. You can flip this around for another important bit of analysis: Good communication doesn't prove the existence of a solid relationship. Nor can good communication be used to solve underlying problems. It can, however, be used to help unearth such problems.

These observations, as they relate to business relationships, are important because they put communication in the proper perspective. While it plays a vital role in managing change, good communication is never by itself the key to successful change management. Furthermore, the presence of good communication should not lure us into lowering our managerial guard, lest we should miss some problems simmering several layers beneath the surface. And again, we can flip things around: Bad communication has never capsized a change effort. If the communication link is down, it's because of some underlying problem. Rehabilitating the change process requires finding and solving that problem.

With all these qualifiers in mind, it's important to recognize that communication still plays a critical role in every effort to manage change. Nearly all the people interviewed for this book cited "good communication" as an essential element. Part of this may arise from the gulf that traditionally has existed between management and workers; employees view communication as the most logical way to bridge that gulf. In addition, change brings uncertainty, and uncertainty brings risk. Communication can reduce uncertainty, thus reducing perceived risk. There are many ways to explain why people consider good communication to be so important. As far as change management is concerned, remember that good communication should be fostered, but it should not be viewed as the ticket to successful implementation.

In the CEI example, Strah's story about union complications at the service center reveals just one occasion when the communication issue surfaced. The importance of good communication came up time and again, and the management team opted for openness. For example, the team didn't attempt to hide any of the facts while unfolding the change. As Zelis put it: "Once the restructuring card decks were delivered to each of their (the supervisors') offices, there were no bones about what our goals were. The supervisors were fully aware we wanted a 10% increase in productivity." As if to back that up, the management team placed emphasis on showing rather than telling employees what was happening. Zelis explained:

> The key ingredient was probably gaining the confidence of the first-line supervisors and the meter-readers. We would deliberately go out early in the morning to each location so that we would be seen. There were some people who advised, "You should wait until the meter-readers are out on the routes before you go into the office." I opposed that. I wanted them to know we were there and to ask questions. That way we were able to communicate very informally that we were there to increase productivity, but that we wouldn't ask them in any way to do something that we ourselves would not be willing to do.

According to Lee Prok, the operations analyst working on the project, the management team fostered a close working relationship with the meter-readers. Team members made clear they weren't above or below the meter-readers, and that they had no intention of pulling a fast one on anyone. Prok described:

> We all had read meters and could relate easily to the work force. We had acquaintances. Nothing gets through more quickly than talking to the readers on an informal, individual basis. You see somebody you read meters with and you say, "Hey, we're not out here to make your life miserable. We're just trying to make sure the readers and the company get a fair deal." That's one of the quickest

ways to get things back to the rank and file.

There were formal channels as well. The seven field supervisors (one for each of the seven service-center locations) served as the liaisons between the management team and the meter-readers. One meter-reader, asked to describe the optimal method for pitching the change plan, described the situation as it actually occurred: "If I were Jim (Warren, a field supervisor) and I had to tell the meter-readers that there was going to be a big change, I would tell them why, what the change consists of, explain it in full detail, and then answer their questions."

In addition to using "communication through showing" and an effective mix of formal and informal channels, the management team made sure they positioned themselves on the receiving end of the communication flow. For instance, during the year following the introduction of hand-held computers, while the management team waited for a year's worth of data to pile up, there was considerable talk among meter-readers of the impending changes. Warren explained management's worries and response:

> One of our chief concerns as we went into the project was, "Boy, we're really going to get hit with some opposition, we may have a major slowdown, we may have some real problems here." We just kind of kept our eyes and ears open. If we saw something developing, we just tried to handle it as we went along. We took our own proactive steps to combat possible problems we thought we might face.

POOLING THE HUMAN RESOURCE

When workers successfully communicate their ideas and feelings about a certain change to management, they move closer to becoming involved in the process. When the manager takes this input and somehow works it into the change, involvement has been achieved. Many veterans of change-management efforts contend that worker involvement is the best way to get workers to "buy into" the change process. Critics contend that worker involvement can become a drag on progress, delaying or even destroying the entire change effort. The key, of course, is to seek and secure an optimal level of involvement. Managers want to get the benefits of worker knowledge while building commitment to the change, yet they shouldn't allow the program to be derailed by conflicting agendas.

The change team at CEI struck the right balance. An important part of their approach involved identifying people whose support, if not involvement, would be vital to the success of the project. By knowing who held sway over the project's fate, the team could add efficiency to the involvement process, lessening the risk of bogging down the change in over-involvement. It was clear, for instance, that the supervisors played an important role. According to Zelis:

> He (the field supervisor) was the guy who was going to have to implement the routing, he was the guy who was going to have to make sure that the newer and longer routes were completed in a day, and of course he was going to be the guy who would take any sarcasm and discontent that would be delivered to him by the meter-readers.

Involvement not only gave supervisors the feeling they had a stake in the change, but also gave the management team a pipeline to expertise. Prok described:

> We (the management team) couldn't really do it; they (the supervisors) had to do it because they have to live with it. I could go in there and change the routes any way I want to, but they had to live with it. It was very important that they were involved in that nitty-gritty part of it. They were the most knowledgeable. I had read meters, so I was fairly familiar, but not to the point where I could tell what part of what route should be combined with another route. That had to be up to the meter-reading supervisor, who was most familiar with the reading area.

Also strategically, in an effort to preempt possible labor problems, Zelis took very conscious steps to involve the unions. He explained:

> When we went into this thing in June, we were cautioned by several union stewards that there was absolutely no doubt that there would be at least ten grievances filed at each location. But that never materialized. In addition to involving the supervisors, we also at each location got a little bit of involvement either from clerks who were close to the bargaining-unit people, or we got some of the bargaining-unit people themselves involved in manipulating the decks and looking at the times. Once they looked at the hard copy and could see what we could see, I think they fully recognized that they could not expect our managers to allow routes to exist that were unreasonably short.

The management team never lost sight of the fact that when all was said and done, meter-readers would be walking the new routes. Thus, the delicate maneuver of striking just the right level of involvement was necessary in dealing with meter-readers, who as a group were quite different from the supervisors. Most notably, there were considerably more meter-readers than supervisors. This heightened the risk of over-involvement, and that was something the management team could not accommodate given their need to implement the change in record time.

In response, management established a form of involvement based more on words than on deeds. "We would get their opinions," Warren explained. "We would simply ask, 'Hey, what do you think about this route, does it need to be cut?' Or, 'How is this route, is it a real gravy route?' We would include them a bit, getting their thoughts on certain things." Communication was established as a two-way process. Meter-readers became involved through the opportunity to voice their opinions and to have those opinions incorporated into the change process.

One worker, an opponent of the change who happened to be temporarily sidelined from his meter-reading job because of an injury, provided an excellent opportunity for the management team to involve this employee level. After being briefed on route completion times, the meter-reader provided suggestions, plowed through project-related paperwork, and reviewed some of the meter-sequencing work that had been completed up to that point. This tangible involvement enabled the management team to neutralize one potential source of opposition. At the same time, it provided other meter-readers with clear evidence that one of their own was helping shape the program.

A FAIR DAY'S WORK

Fairness is a sensitive issue to employees in all areas of an organization. Perhaps more than any other department, however, operations often becomes a battleground in which different groups pursue different definitions of fairness. Unfortunately, much of the writing on change management neglects this theme. The likely reason: Fairness seems too vague to be worked into specific managerial tactics. What is fairness? How do you achieve it? Is it possible, or even desirable, to be completely fair to all people? Plain and simple answers are elusive. Perhaps the best way to understand fairness, and the importance of it, is to look at fairness in action.

The change process at CEI provides a good example. There, management faced the difficult task of increasing the work load on many routes, which created an excellent opportunity for fairness watchdogs to cry foul. To squelch the charge right from the start, management presented the new system in a "give and take" context. Zelis explained:

> There were some suburban routes that grew very rapidly and got away from us. The routes simply were too long. The workers saw an honest effort on our part to shave those routes down, and we did so dramatically in some cases. We took a very fair approach. We looked at the times. We could tell when a particular account had been read. If we saw that at a quarter to four in the afternoon a particular route could not be completed, we chopped the remainder of the route out and attached that portion to a shorter route.
>
> At the same time, when the data indicated that a route was being completed too early, we would be up-front and honest with them. "Let's face it, fellas, you all know we're paid until 4:30, so we're going to increase the size of the route so the company gets a fair day's work for a fair day's pay. And just as important, the work will

> be distributed equitably between readers. No reader will be assigned easy routes while others struggle with oversized routes."

Communication played an essential role in conveying fairness. The management team's pitch: Sure, you won't be finishing up early anymore, but neither will you risk having to spend your last couple of hours hustling to finish. The message was easily understood and easily conveyed, and management wisely made a practice of stating it time and again. By frequently reminding supervisors and meter-readers of the fairness issue, and of how the changes would increase fairness, management nipped much of the skepticism in the bud. Management's case was strengthened by the good wage CEI pays its meter-readers. A perception of "fair pay" seemed to create a positive atmosphere, perhaps making workers more receptive to the change.

All of this makes it sound very simple: Tell employees the change is fair, and sit back while they nod in agreement. In fact, there are other forces at work that determine the credibility level. For one, there's the matter of who communicates with the workers. If the change, and the fairness issue, are explained by someone who lacks credibility or is not respected by workers, the change may be perceived as being unfair. More seriously, if the pitch is made by someone who has a rough record in terms of fairness, workers will likely reject the person and the proposed change. It usually doesn't matter whether the change, taken by itself, is arguably fair. The identify of the messenger can powerfully impact how the message is received.

For one meter-reader at CEI, the persuasive factor was field supervisor Jim Warren. Warren was well-known as a veteran meter-reader and well-liked as a personable guy who could talk comfortably with people at all levels. For meter-readers, it meant a great deal that Warren himself had faced vicious dogs, irate homeowners, and oversized routes. He had been there, on the front lines, doing what they did every day. When Warren stood before his crew and explained the change that was about to unfold, his veteran status carried more weight than anything he could have said. One meter-reader recalled:

> I think everybody understood Jim because he used to be out here doing this. He knows all the tricks of the trade.

> He knows you might finish a route early one day. He knows all that. Coming from Jim, it was OK because he knows....
>
> (Asked how the news would have been received had it been delivered by an outsider:) I would have said, "How can you tell me about the route when I'm out on the route and you've never been out there?"

Another fairness issue can involve differing agendas. Two managers may have separate views of what's fair, and this can evolve into conflicting messages to workers. If these messages persist, workers begin questioning management's commitment to the change. At CEI, this issue surfaced when one manager began pushing for excessive productivity improvements. The manager, unfamiliar with meter-reading, set route-size goals so high that even the best readers would have been unable to reach them. The four members of the management team felt the addition would tip the fairness balance far in the workers' disfavor. Further, if a route could not be completed in one day, a return trip would duplicate travel and delay billing. Team leader Zelis responded by isolating the case and assuring the manager that his readers would be productive. Zelis very consciously kept the matter out of the range of workers and other managers.

Asked to describe their philosophies of change, most members of the CEI team highlighted fairness and equity as major components. Warren, probably recalling his own days as a meter-reader, said his own philosophy involves:

> ...being honest with the worker and trying to give the worker an even break. Being in management, we expect certain things from the workers, but we don't want to expect more than we'd expect of ourselves. Be honest and up-front with him, just expecting an honest day's work for an honest day's pay.

THE "GAME PAGE"

Different definitions of fairness aren't the only source of problems that can arise from managerial layers. More broadly, each manager can bring a different agenda to the change process. This can mean different goals, different approaches, and different reasons for the change. Yet a common agenda is essential in order to focus managers' energy and show employees that management unanimously supports the change plan. As Prok put it: "Everybody has to be on the same game page in order for any type of project to be successful."

Prok speaks from experience. He and his fellow management team members encountered the agenda issue when they became deeply involved in the meter-reading change. One manager, as already noted, wanted to shoot for even higher productivity increases by packing more accounts onto each route. Another manager went the other way, advocating less restructuring. These managers were one level above the field supervisors—a powerful position in terms of being able to sway supervisors' opinions of the change. It didn't seem to matter that Zelis had the backing of the vice president for operations, who had been the chief standard-bearer in bringing electronic meter-reading to CEI. According to Zelis:

> I was convincing the first-line supervisors, and our team was convinced (of the merits of the change), but the next level of supervision up (the middle-level managers) was not working closely enough with me to be convinced. Also, they weren't close enough to our executives to know how strongly they supported the project. They were in-between, and they weren't getting solid communications.

Although these middle-level managers didn't have specific responsibilities in implementing the plan, they did control some very tangible parts of the overall work environment. Zelis described:

> They have direct influence over the appraisals of the first-line supervisors. If you don't keep that guy well-informed, and he's giving his first-line supervisor instructions that oppose the instructions I'm giving the first-line supervisor, then you've got conflict. And that first-line supervisor has been caught between his manager and me, with me representing an executive officer. As a result, the supervisor doesn't know which way to go. "Gee, should I make that route longer or shouldn't I? My boss says no, and he is

> the guy who does my appraisal. But then, John Zelis is representing the vice president, who will review my appraisal and approve any salary increase."

This happened in part because middle-level managers lacked a short-term role in directly shaping the change process. The management team looked to them primarily for support, which could be classified as indirect involvement. With the new rate structure weighing on their minds, the managers may have been preoccupied with speedy implementation. This seemed to generate an operational myopia in which management dealt only with meter-readers, field supervisors, and others whose jobs would be affected most directly by the new system. The level above field supervisor ended up getting cut out of the process.

Looking back critically at the change process, Zelis described what he would do differently to avoid this problem. His words further reveal why a common agenda can be difficult to create.

> I would take that level of supervision (middle-level managers), gather them together in one meeting, and I would have our vice president speak to them directly about his goals. As it was, the information did go down through the hierarchy, but it was imperfect information because most of it was carried verbally and indirectly. More simply put, I recognized the need to communicate with readers and first-line supervisors but failed to make certain that middle-level managers understood the goals as well as the restructuring process.

CONCLUSION

The two phases of change at Cleveland Electric Illuminating Co. involved mainly technical issues; change had negligible impact on the organization's culture. Recalling the simple grid introduced at the beginning of Part II, with "culture" as the y-axis and "technical" as the x-axis, we see that the CEI case fits in the southeast quadrant. The immediate implication: Change could be implemented relatively quickly.

At CEI, adoption of hand-held computers and implementation

of the newly structured route system were pushed forward expeditiously. Observers could even argue that haste triggered some of the problems. For instance, middle-level management seemed to be neglected. Also, quickness aggravated certain technical problems; a glitch affecting one service location invariably affected the six other locations. There was insufficient time for testing and debugging. Of course, as we have seen, the management team needed to work quickly to stay several paces ahead of the impending rate change.

Overall, the entire change effort proved successful. The management team used a mix of formal and informal communication channels to inform workers of the change. At the same time, they made a point of creating a two-way communication flow, ensuring that they could pick up employee feedback. In terms of involvement, management achieved the necessary balance, involving key people yet not getting bogged down in over-involvement. Only with middle-level managers did the management team fail to foster communication and involvement.

The team displayed a marked sensitivity to fairness. This may have emerged from their own supervisory experience and their backgrounds in meter-reading. Management moved carefully to ensure that the changes were fair, and they thoroughly communicated this fact to the workers. Meanwhile, the attempt to form a common agenda proved only partially successful. Two key groups, meter-readers and first-line supervisors, were successfully persuaded to buy into the program. But again, some members of middle management wielded opposing agendas because of incomplete communication and isolation from the process. The management team realized this early enough to take appropriate action and keep the change on schedule.

4

PROFILE: CULTURAL CHANGE AT NUCOR MACHINED PRODUCTS

Kenneth Iverson, CEO of Nucor Corp., was looking to acquire a machined-products company when he learned about General Bearing. The acquisition prospect seemed perfectly tailored to Nucor's need for machining technology. By buying an existing company instead of building one from scratch, which was Nucor's typical course of action, Nucor could speed its entry into a new market. The plant produced unground steel bearings, semi-ground bearings, automotive bearings, and machined steel parts.

Nucor purchased General Bearing, located in Wilson, North Carolina, in December 1986. Nucor's managers then began the task of integrating the plant and its 300 workers into the Nucor culture. That, it seemed, was when the real work began. The cultural transformation required a 180-degree turn in the norms and values of former General Bearing employees.

Nucor certainly didn't have a shortage of money to launch and lead the change. The billion-dollar company is the ninth largest steel maker in the country and among the most profitable. But money and size had nothing to do with this particular change process. At General Bearing, now called Nucor Machined Products, the wheels of change had been rusted immovable by 18 years of strict top-down management.

Larry Townsend joined General Bearing just 20 days before the Nucor purchase. (Because the acquisition was well in the works by that time, he was interviewed by Nucor before being hired.) As general manager of the new Nucor Machined Products, Townsend was given the task of completely changing the operation's culture. He provided this nutshell analysis of the situation:

> Everyone here had grown up under what was known as a benevolent dictatorship. No decisions were permitted to be made here; all the shots were called at the corporate headquarters in New York, including purchasing decisions. We were really starting from ground zero in terms of converting from a truly top-down management organization to a Nucor bottom-up organization.

To understand the breadth of the change, one needs to understand the Nucor culture. A simple two-sentence description might read: Nucor thrives on bottom-up management, assuring that employees and their ideas are fully utilized so that customers receive top-quality products. Customers are the most important external group, and employees are the most important internal group because they support customers. Iverson, Nucor's CEO, added the following detail:

> One feature is that we believe in few management layers. In the whole company there are only four: the foreman, the department head, the general managers of the divisions, and the corporate office. We believe in as little staff as you can probably get by with. Our total corporate office is 17 people, including clerical help. We believe very strongly in incentives, and everybody in the company has a significant part of their compensation based either on the success of the company or on production above a certain standard. We believe also that these incentives should not be subjective, so they are all "formulized." We have no discretionary bonuses anywhere in the company.

As evidence, Iverson presents a December 1988 letter that accompanied a $500 check to each employee. The letter reads:

> Our Company has a policy that all employees should share in the Company's success. As part of that policy the Company contributes about 10 cents out of every dollar

> of earnings before taxes to the Employees Profit Sharing Plan. For 1988 we will have record earnings and the amount contributed to Profit Sharing will be significantly greater than last year.
>
> The Board of Directors has decided to make a special early cash payment of a portion of the 1988 Profit Sharing. On December 15th each employee will receive $500....
>
> This is the fourth time our Company has made a special payment of this type. I am sure you all realize that in order to do so the Company must have exceptional earnings. We have divisions that need to improve their earnings.
>
> We must all work together to produce our products efficiently so that we can sell them profitably in the marketplace....

Nearly all the features of the Nucor environment had been conspicuously absent from General Bearing, underscoring the complexity of the change process. Yet Townsend remained clear on his mission: "You have a couple basic premises that you have to implement. One is that manufacturing is in fact responsible for everything. Also, you have to structure the operation with a bonus program so it's effective, so it allows employees to be rewarded for what they do. Those are the real keys of the change, but in that is a huge arena."

With these premises in mind, Townsend launched the change effort. He began by restructuring the operation to match Nucor's organization. This involved changes in policies and personnel. For example, Townsend reduced by half the number of department managers. Also, just four months after the acquisition, Nucor introduced a plant-wide bonus program. Meanwhile, Townsend kept close tabs on managerial personalities. In some cases, key people simply couldn't adopt the new culture and were let go.

This was the easy part. It was another matter entirely to persuade people to adopt the new norms and values implicit in these tangible changes. When this chapter was written, about three years into the change process at Nucor Machined Products, management reported being only halfway to its cultural goals for the division. This is how Townsend described the challenges that continue to surface in converting from a top-down to a bottom-up management system:

> Most people don't want the responsibility that goes with the ability to make their own decisions and guide their own destinies. It's a whole lot easier for someone to do what they're told than it is to tell themselves what to do. It's safer; there's no risk.
>
> Nucor encourages people to take risks, to try different things, to be on the leading edge of technology, to try things that have never been tried before, to make mistakes because you can't make all good decisions. And those things are tough—for employees and especially for supervisors—who have had it pounded into their heads that they are not to think.
>
> Now we say to a supervisor: "This is your product, these are your people, these are your machines, this is your profit center. You do what you have to do to make it work, to make money at it." That's something people don't easily grab hold of. Supervisors and hourly people have never been given an opportunity to see cost information. Now they see it all. We ask them to control their inventory, to ship products on time, to control scrap. We don't tell them what they have to do. We tell them what the expectations are and tell them it's up to them how to do it and what to do. And that's what's difficult wherever you go. That gets to the heart of managing the change process.

The process is still underway at Nucor Machined Products, providing an excellent example of cultural change—the type of change positioned in the northwest quadrant of the change grid presented earlier. The process involves a relatively small amount of technical change, but the complexity involved in successfully changing people's norms and values requires a great deal of time. Predictably, some of the issues related to cultural change differ from those related to technical change. These issues, as they come into play in the case of Nucor Machined Products, are described in the following analysis.

CHANGING THE FRAMEWORK

Companies are people, as the saying goes. But companies also are rules, policies, and procedures. They also are organization charts. Even the most free-wheeling companies have some type of structural framework in which they produce goods and services. At Nucor, all the divisional general managers meet three times a year. According to Iverson, one of these meetings deals solely with corporate policies and practices. "It's all sorts of things—vacations, holidays, sick days," Iverson said. "We have some really basic things: We don't allow the title 'assistant to.' Everybody has to wear the same color hard hat. You get no assigned parking spaces. There are no company cars, no company airplanes, no executive dining rooms."

Structural issues are especially relevant to a discussion of change when the change involves culture, because structure provides tangible cues to the type of culture existing in an organization. At Nucor, Townsend launched the change process by dismantling many features of the old company and building new policies and procedures in their place. The new structure affirmed and conveyed the tone of the Nucor culture, providing employees with visible reminders of the new way of thinking.

For instance, shortly after his arrival, Townsend ended an old General Bearing practice by eliminating assigned parking spaces. Assigned spaces violated Nucor's culture, which affirms that employees are equal players in the organization. In addition, the company set aside four visitor spaces. In the Nucor culture, suppliers are highly valued. The specially reserved parking spaces provided tangible evidence of this one aspect of the new culture. Another change related to personnel: Performance appraisals were eliminated. "Our philosophy is that you tell people where they're at all the time," Townsend explained. "It shouldn't come as a surprise if they (employees) have a problem."

These policy changes were accompanied by changes in personnel structure. Townsend noted some of the major alterations:

> Nucor limits the number of department managers you typically have to four or five in a division, no matter how big the division is. When I got here we had eight people reporting to me—all department managers. Now we have four. That change took place fairly quickly in terms of

> defining department managers, but I still had people working directly for me. As we changed the organization down to four managers, we eliminated production control, product engineering, and the quality manager as separate functions.

Under the Nucor culture, "manufacturing is king," Townsend noted. At Nucor Machined Products, this meant that engineering responsibilities were given to manufacturing. Production control and inventory management became the responsibility of supervisors. Industrial engineers were phased out. All of these structural changes underscored the cultural emphasis on manufacturing, showing this fact in clear terms and making it a part of everyday operational life. The goal: to give manufacturing most of the say in determining the operation's destiny. Today, of the 300 people employed at the machined-products division, only 20 work in administration.

Looking back on the change process, Townsend observed that change would have been much more difficult to achieve if workers had been unionized. None of Nucor's divisions is unionized, which allows considerably more room for the types of incentive programs that figure so prominently in the company's compensation structure. This managerial freedom enabled Townsend to get a quick start in transforming the culture. The fact that the transformation is only partially completed suggests just how difficult the cultural change process can be for managers who operate in rigidly unionized environments.

CHANGING PEOPLE

When hearing talk about the structure of an organization, we usually think of inanimate features like policies. Rounding out the picture, however, are people. The personalities that make up an organization, especially the personalities of influential people like managers and supervisors, have a positive or negative impact on the change process. People either pick up on the new culture and begin to foster it, or they cling to the old culture and stifle the new one right from the start.

This has important implications for managers who are directing a change process. They should avoid assuming, for example, that a skeptical supervisor cannot single-handedly jeopardize the effort. One influential person can indeed sway the opinions of many others and, in so doing, stall the change process. An adequate response often requires training, informal and formal communication, and sufficient time to allow the skeptic to see the benefits of the new culture. Sometimes, special tactics must be used. Other times, the employee must be pulled out of the position.

Townsend found himself drawing from a full menu of approaches as he headed into this second and more difficult phase of change. The next section in this chapter discusses how he communicated the change to employees. As for removing people from the operation, of the 11 manufacturing supervisors, only two remained in their positions two years after the acquisition. The production manager, an 18-year veteran of General Bearing, was replaced one year after Nucor took over.

More than any other employee, the production manager showed how a single person can hobble an entire change effort. The manager seemed unable to adopt the new culture, and his prominent and influential position made him a significant threat to the cultural changes. Townsend recalled:

> When I got here, we were shipping anything and everything we could produce. I told him (the production manager) and the quality manager, "Thou shalt not ship anything that's not top quality." It was virtually ignored because, in the mind of the production manager, how do you keep shipping and making your dollars if you can't ship everything you make? He and the quality manager both said, "Yeah, we're doing that." But as it turned out, they didn't. When our new production manager came here, I didn't even have to tell him. He discovered the problem and stopped it.
>
> Another example deals with inventory. We had a lot of in-process inventory, and we kept finding that a lot of it wasn't of any value. I figured, we're going to take the hit in 1987, put that behind us, scrap it, and we're done with it.... But they didn't want to do it because he (the production manager) was hanging onto it just in case—so if something blipped in the production process, he'd always have that to go, even if it wasn't any good.

Townsend's new production manager, Jake Schmidt, was a Nucor veteran brought in from a Utah plant. Well-schooled in Nucor ways, Schmidt wasted little time in making sure the production operation matched the Nucor culture. In the process, Schmidt employed some special tactics. One of them involved using pride as a motivating force. He described:

> The people who were purported to have the most experience in a particular area, who had the aura of being the most knowledgeable in that area, were the ones who had the most to lose if change were to occur. They were the ones who came along dragging their feet....
>
> Pride is a big player. You'd look at the newer people, those with the least amount of authority, differently. You could get them to take pride. You'd say, "Hey, you are new, now is your time to take over and to really learn this. You could take leaps and bounds ahead of some of these people who have been here for years but haven't taken the opportunity to learn." To entrenched people, you had to say, "Look, these people are going to take off and go around you and continue to go if you don't realize that change is going to be a part of your life around here. You're going to have to accept this."

Even though approaches like these pushed forward the change process, Townsend said he would do things a bit differently if given the chance to repeat the first two years. One example: He would make even more personnel changes earlier into the change process.

> You can't just say to manufacturing, "It's your responsibility," and have it happen. They don't even understand what you're talking about. "What do you mean it's my responsibility? I don't know anything at this point. I don't know what my requirements are, I don't know what my costs are, I don't know who my people are in some cases." So you can say those things, and I said them, but in reality they have to accept it before change has occurred, and they don't accept it all up front.
>
> It's an evolution. You take little bits at a time, and they start doing it, and you work with them and nurture

> that, and you get them good at it. For instance, take financial reports. It's fairly complicated to know what your return on assets is, what your profitability is, and so on. It's an undertaking just to get them to understand that, let alone to make it better, because if they don't understand the numbers they can't possibly make it better.

From his vantage point as chief executive officer of Nucor, Iverson has his own retrospective view on the early stages:

> We really approached it in the same way we would approach any division in that we delegated to Larry Townsend the authorities that go with that position. Perhaps if we had not delegated so much we could have found a way to move it a little bit faster into our culture. But we really elected not to do so. We did supply accounting people and standards people from this office (corporate headquarters) who spent a great deal of time there, kind of aiding him, setting up the reports in a manner that was the type we'd like to receive. But outside of that, it was really trying to effect it by going through him rather than our dealing directly with the employees.

The purchase of General Bearing marked Nucor's first acquisition—a big departure from the company's typical practice of building new divisions from the ground up. The fact that corporate headquarters gave its newest division (and newest general manager) an average amount of managerial attention may have stalled the early phase of the change process; the division required more than the usual input given to each division. The replacement of the production manager a year after the acquisition seemed to be a turning point that invigorated the cultural transformation.

MORE SHOW THAN TELL

Culture, as we have noted, deals with people's norms and values. Cultural change thus involves changing some fairly hazy concepts. Technical change, by comparison, deals with the clear concept of what people do and how they do it. Considering all this, it's no surprise culture can be difficult to explain and understand.

But few doubt the fact that culture is pervasive and powerful. An employee may not be able to articulate with policy-book precision that suppliers are consider vital to the operation, but he or she knows that the first four parking spaces are for visitors only. Imbedded in this is an important managerial lesson: Culture is best conveyed in terms of actions and symbols rather than words.

Up to this point, we have seen how changes in structure and personnel were used to push along the change process at Nucor Machined Products. These have significant value in communicating the new culture. But communication, which is so important in allaying fears and converting employees to the new culture, must be a broader effort that continues evenly as the change unfolds. The optimal approach seems to be a small amount of "telling" followed by a large and consistent campaign of "showing."

When Nucor acquired the operation, there was no major announcement that a cultural change would take place. "You can announce a physical change, but you can't announce a philosophical change," Townsend theorizes. Even so, Townsend communicated directly with his staff, highlighting the main features of the Nucor culture. He and the staff then communicated directly with the supervisors. The supervisors were expected to deliver the message to remaining levels. The approach may have been a bit too informal. As the management team at Cleveland Electric Illuminating Co. discovered, messages sometimes get garbled as they travel through the managerial layers—even if the number of layers is small, as at Nucor. Distortion can rewrite the message or, worse, create the perception that management is not committed to the change.

As for fears regarding job security, verbal assurances are insufficient, Townsend believes. "It (fear) is there, and until you demonstrate that there's no reason to have it, it's going to remain." In other words: Actions speak louder than words. At Nucor Machined Products, a profit-sharing plan left over from General Bearing days was a sticking point for some employees who otherwise might have been more open to the new culture. Management responded with action. Townsend recalled:

> I think it took a year for them to get comfortable that Nucor policies are much more beneficial to employees than the old policies were. There was a profit-sharing

> program from General Bearing which took roughly a year-and-a-half to get closed out and paid out. Their overriding fear was that they were going to lose their money. That was paramount in their mind. Since we've paid that out, there hasn't been any overriding issue that keeps people from focusing on their jobs.

Dismantling such obstacles prepared employees for the new culture. So did the changes affecting structure and personnel. But successful change required a much more powerful tool for fully reversing the forces of top-down management. At Nucor Machined Products, as at all Nucor divisions, this tool took the form of a bonus program.

Implementation of a program four months after acquisition gave Townsend an excellent opportunity to back up corporate claims with indisputable dollars. The system consisted of bonus groups, which were responsible for distinct areas of the operation. Improvement ideas were to emerge from each group, thus creating a teamwork approach to problem-solving. Bonuses would be awarded accordingly, distributed to group members rather than to individuals. Townsend used the program to reach employees directly, perhaps marking the actual time the full-scale change effort was launched.

> I personally reviewed the program with each employee: how it worked, how the standards were established, what effect they could have, that we were in fact turning over the responsibility for making more bonuses to them. I pointed out that it's not my job to improve their bonus; it's their job. Then we started paying it and reporting it, so everyone knew. And again, it's an evolution. Somebody does real well and everybody says, "Gee, that's fantastic, what do I have to do to do that?" And so you start working with different groups to give them ideas on how they can become involved.

Following the start of the bonus program, Townsend worked continuously to fuel the bottom-up style. The process wasn't marked by occasional speeches or sporadic strolls through the plant. Rather, the effort became an ongoing campaign that continues to this day. At every opportunity, Townsend displays the Nucor way by consulting with supervisors and production workers. "They bring things up and I say, 'What do you think, what are you going to do about that? I can't tell you what to do, you tell me what you're going to do.'" Production manager Schmidt uses the same approach. He explained:

> I pushed the decision-making as far down the ladder as humanly possible. I would let them be responsible. If they came in and said something wouldn't work, I'd say, "Fine, why wouldn't it work? What do you plan to do about it?"
>
> This requires persistence and time. But on top of that, you have to believe and you have to do what you say you're going to do. You have to show that the employee is the most important person on the floor, that the employee does make a difference, that the employee does make the quality, that the employee does have a say in what the employee does. You not only have to believe that and talk that, you have to act that.

As production employees responded to the bonus program, following the lead of people like Townsend and Schmidt, improvement ideas slowly began to emerge. The bonus program seemed to be working, but was it working as well as it could? Management asked this question in early 1989 and became convinced the program was not reaching its full potential. They concluded that the bonus groups, each consisting on average of 25 people, were too big; individuals didn't feel they could have a significant impact on the fortunes of the group. And from this, the perception grew that individuals had little personal control over their own bonuses. Employees were being asked to control their own destinies, yet they did not have a mechanism that effectively enabled them to do so. Management responded with a mid-course adjustment, reducing the average bonus-group size. Each group now numbers five to 10 employees.

All the while, Townsend has conveyed the Nucor culture by using himself as a model:

> I get pretty involved in the technical change process. As a result, I get involved with people. They come to understand through this that I'm just somebody else. I don't have any problem getting my hands dirty. Right now

> we're installing a new line, and it's really my baby. I designed it, and I'm determined to make it work. I'm out there working on the pieces of equipment. People see that and they recognize they can talk to me because I'm just somebody else. I'm no more important than they are.

With the change process several years along, the two-way communication flow, which is so much a part of the Nucor culture, is being heard on the plant floor. According to Townsend:

> I think we're at the point now where most employees, if their boss tells them to do something that they think is wrong, they'll wave the flag and say, "Time out, I don't think that's right." And there's a fairly large percentage who, if their supervisor says do it anyway, will use our formal open-door policy and go to the production manager or to me and say, "This is what's going on and I don't think it's right, would you get involved in it?"

Another good sign are the annual dinners hosted by the general manager. At each, 30 to 50 employees spend an evening with Townsend—with their supervisors noticeably absent. Employees are encouraged to speak their minds no matter how critical their comments. The dinners are a tradition at all Nucor divisions. In 1987, Townsend's dinner guests were markedly quiet. Still accustomed to the old style, most felt more comfortable listening than speaking. All that changed in 1988. A pleased Townsend reported that employees engaged in a critical discussion of the operation.

CONCLUSION

Townsend can point to important signs that the change process is on track at Nucor Machined Products. Office staff and expenses have fallen 35% while productivity has climbed 15%. Sales for 1988 were 20% above the previous year's level. Manufacturing cost has been reduced as a percentage of sales by 2.5%. Meanwhile, the old staff-function structure has given way to a system in which first-line supervision is the operational centerpiece.

The signs are good, but the cultural change process is far from complete. The Nucor culture is readily understood at the plant, yet not all people have adopted the norms and values as their own. The bonus program and other tangible components of the culture will keep the change process moving forward. It seems time is needed more than anything else to complete the transformation.

Taking a critical look, we can debate whether management set an optimal pace for instilling the new culture in the old organization. Critics would point out that Nucor headquarters held back the change effort by not giving its new division enough special treatment. Others would note that this was the first time Nucor made an acquisition—and had to deal with all the cultural baggage brought along by a different organization. The managerial pace early on suggests that managers at all levels were learning how to adapt to the situation. Still others would note that it goes against Nucor's culture to mingle too much in the affairs of its divisions. With its lean structure, Nucor is a model of decentralization, and excessive corporate involvement in the new division would have added more time to the change.

Much of the change involved molding the structure of the newly acquired company to fit the Nucor culture. This involved inanimate components like policies. It also covered personnel, prompting a major thinning of the operation's managerial ranks. Meanwhile, the general manager dealt directly with personalities, removing people whose adherence to the old culture threatened the change effort. This became most obvious in the case of the production manager. In other situations, management used special tactics, like presenting the change to new employees as an opportunity for advancement.

Communication threaded its way through the entire process. Structural changes had a definite communication value, helping to define the Nucor culture for plant employees. More directly, Townsend and Schmidt persistently worked to create an atmosphere in which each employee would want to contribute. They made a point of encouraging two-way communication, which led employees to dig up their own solutions. They also became directly involved in plant work, showing employees not only the equality of all workers, but also affirming through action the idea that every worker should make a direct contribution to the operation. The bonus program, a main driving force of the culture, provided formal proof that the company valued bottom-up initiative.

5

PROFILE: TECHNICAL AND CULTURAL CHANGE AT REYNOLDS METALS CO.

Reynolds Metals Co. is best known by consumers for its aluminum foil, but the company is much more. Its operations, fueled by massive quantities of raw materials, labor, and equipment, churn out hundreds of products for consumer and industrial customers worldwide. One example is the Alloys Sheet and Plate Plant, which employs 2,350 people in Sheffield, Alabama. There, the "hot mill" produces enormous sheets of thick aluminum for the industrial market. The hot line department is manned by 130 production people and serviced by an equal number of maintenance employees.

In 1984, Reynolds invested in a program to improve the maintenance management function at the hot mill. For years, maintenance had been extremely reactive, with maintenance craftsmen spending most of their time simply doing whatever needed to be done at the moment. The new program aimed to make maintenance more of a planned undertaking. Reynolds viewed a proactive system as a way to reduce the amount of equipment downtime while improving maintenance quality. If the program succeeded, it would be installed in other areas of the plant.

Reynolds hired a consulting firm to develop and implement the full maintenance management system. A consultant spent about six months at the plant, working with Reynolds employees to tailor the system. The complete program had many components. For instance, it established a system of standard work times for specific maintenance jobs. Using the system, maintenance job planners would assign a standard time to each actual job when processing a work order. This would simplify the development of workable weekly schedules. In addition, the planner would draft a job plan for each individual maintenance job and ensure the availability of necessary parts, materials, and repair equipment. These job plans would then be used by maintenance craftsmen in making the repairs.

The change process involved technical *and* cultural aspects. Technically, the system included specific methods for planning jobs, developing and applying standard times, planning major projects, and so forth. At the same time, inherent in the program was an attempt to change major norms and values of employees. A proactive approach to maintenance management would replace about 40 years of responding to problems as they arose. The program took job planning out of the hands of craftsmen and supervisors, and made it the responsibility of a separate group of job planners. In addition, it required craftsmen to begin using Time Distribution Cards to record their daily utilization of time. This information, manipulated with the standard times on a new computer system, would produce yet another new feature: management reports tracking department trends like efficiency, coverage, performance, and effectiveness. Such measuring sticks had never before been such a pervasive part of the work environment.

The sweeping nature of the change required skillful management. On the one hand, the situation called for a visionary who could rally support for the program among the skeptical and somewhat fearful workers. On the other hand, the program required a master of detail who could implement the many technical components. The consultant attempted to support both roles and complete both missions, crunching everything into a six-month time frame.

Jim Ogborne became plant superintendent in 1985. Reflecting on the change process, he cited resistance from several key groups:

> From a maintenance viewpoint, it was a hard sell. Not only was maintenance management not really convinced it was the thing to do, because they like to plan out of their back pocket, but it was not perceived well by craft people (the maintenance workers). They preferred to have a lot of people roaming the mill looking for trouble, and there's probably some merit to that in some operations.

> If you have a maintenance system that really does work, however, you don't need people roaming in the mill because those kinds of breakdowns don't happen—you have time in which you plan to fix things every day, every weekend, every month, and every year. And if you plan that job right, and you know the things that will haunt you, you don't have to worry about shutting down the mill during run time. But they were convinced we couldn't run these mills without people roaming all around and handling these things at their discretion, and without having to deal with all the paperwork. They didn't like it; they resisted it.
>
> On the other side, the production people didn't like it. There were two reasons. The production line foreman didn't like it because of the paperwork he had to deal with. He had to write work orders. The management-level people in production didn't like it because now they had to sort things by priority, and that means choices. Production people don't like choices; they want everything now. You can't have that in a maintenance planning system. You have to have priorities.

The change process unfolded in several phases. First, the consultant communicated the program to supervisors, planners, and hourly employees. Then they were trained in some aspects of the system. Planners received the bulk of the training, which was based on a course provided by the consulting firm. Next, in step-by-step fashion, every component of the program was developed in an effort to fill the maintenance needs of the hot-mill operation. The consultant, working with a group of Reynolds employees, assembled the standard times. A computerized maintenance management system was installed, automating such maintenance functions as work-order generation and tracking, job planning, equipment history, and management reports.

The maintenance craftsmen recognized early on that the program meant significant changes in the way they accomplished work. One of the craftsmen, a hot-line machinist, offered the following description of the new maintenance management system. His comments hint at the resistance that came to characterize many employees' attitudes and feelings toward the program.

> The work was going to be the same. They were just asking for a different approach to it. It would be a schedule-type approach. What they wanted to do was plan a job. Before, when you were on the job, you just went to the job and did it. When you go to a job now, it's supposed to be laid out for you....
>
> A craftsman, he's supposed to have enough pride in his work and enough know-how without someone telling him the steps to take. I believe the orientation would have been better if they had asked, "What do you think it's going to take to do this job?" Instead, they just laid it out and said, "This is what we're going to do."

No, change didn't come easy. In fact, the process continues to unfold to this day. According to Temple Brown, vice president for research and development, about 50% of the program's original goals have been reached. (At the time of the interviews for this chapter, Brown was vice president for operations.)

Recalling the grid introduced at the beginning of Part II, we can confidently position the change in the northeast quadrant: It involves major cultural and technical issues. Managing such a comprehensive change requires considerable time and effort. Much of what remains unaccomplished at the hot-line department involves the cultural component. Resistance relates more to norms and values rather than to operational concerns like how to fill out a time card. The following analysis, like the change itself, is complex. It takes a wide-angle look at the major technical and cultural issues that surfaced during the change process.

SELLING TO TOUGH CUSTOMERS

By embarking on the maintenance management program, Reynolds injected considerable uncertainty into the operations environment. The unions immediately picked up on this and quietly began to build a wall of opposition. One union dug up information that seemed to link the consulting firm with union-busting. The literature soon found its way to a bulletin board, and employees began to talk. As it turned out, the charges resulted from a simple case of mistaken identity: The information related to a different firm that happened to have a similar name. But even when the real story was told, suspicion remained. "You can't stop a rumor," observed a hot-line maintenance supervisor. "That's what we were up against. It took a year to show them (the hourly workers) that they (the consultants) were not here to break the union." The proof came over time as workers saw for themselves that union-breaking simply was not on the agenda in any way, shape, or form.

The general foreman for hot-line production described the collective response this way:

> There's more resistance to change in a large plant. The larger the plant, the stronger the union influence—and the more resistance to change you're going to have. When management comes in and says, "We're considering changing this," you've immediately created an area of suspicion with some of your people. You've got to convince them that the change is necessary for the good and welfare not only of the company, but also of them as individuals.

Against this backdrop of skepticism, the consultant communicated details about the new program to all employees. He used a direct approach, explaining what the program would consist of and how it would work. A veteran of such programs, the consultant may have assumed that the merits of the system would be obvious and quickly accepted. While some employees recognized certain benefits, others remained anxious and unconvinced. Most felt the program was being pushed on them. Others thought the sales pitch lacked sufficient proof that the results of the change would be worth the effort. The production general foreman said he believes communication would have been more effective if there had been more emphasis on showing, rather than telling, the benefits.

> I would have identified other areas in the plant, or certain competitors, that are successfully using it. I understand the Japanese have something like this, and it's working well. Then I would institute it department by department. I would go into these areas and identify the leaders. Then I would literally put these strong people in that environment for a short period of time, if I could. I

> would show them the system and how it works. And then I'd spend quite a bit of time educating people on why this thing is necessary and what we hope to achieve....
>
> You need to relate the benefits to the individual. For example, show him that if we institute this program, we can stockpile bearings for a particular application more efficiently and cheaply because we'll have background data. Then we can forecast what we need six months down the road. You need to convince people and use the things they're familiar with and interested in.

Temple Brown, the vice president based at the Reynolds headquarters in Richmond, Virginia, acknowledged some of the difficulties of selling the program. While plant management seemed committed, they didn't fully understand the program's intricacies. This lack of understanding prevented full commitment. Brown, like the production general foreman, also believes early communication should have taken the form of a full-scale sales pitch to show employees why the program was worth the effort. He explained: "You're talking meetings, you're talking success stories, you're talking examples where you let them see it first hand. Let them talk to people who have put it in, let them see it in operation, let them see that it's successful."

Another important issue deals with the accuracy of communication and the expectations that arise from it. If employees are told to expect a certain outcome, and the actual outcome is different, the communicator's credibility can be seriously undermined. If the actual outcome is less desirable than what was predicted, the communicator can be perceived as unfair.

At the hot-line operation, workers picked up on certain statements they later perceived to be untrue. What was said did not translate into what they later saw. In the early communications, expectations may have been set too high in hopes of attracting immediate support. Or, the consultant simply may have been guilty of excessive optimism. Whatever the case, workers used this gap between expectations and perceived outcome to question the consultant's credibility. In retrospect, this may have undermined all future communications. The hot-line maintenance general foreman, who worked as a front-line supervisor when the program was launched, recalled:

> When they brought this program out, it was put to the people—and I'm talking salaried supervisors, too—that there's going to be less paperwork, it's going to be easier on the salaried supervisors. Some people said, "Hey, all I've got to do is come out on the job, my material will be here, there won't be any paperwork, all I've got to do is say here it is, you go here and you go there, follow up." That was not the case. In fact, it's more paperwork, it's more documentation—all to get better records.
>
> We should have assembled all the salaried supervisors first and said, "Look, this is what we have, it's a good program. It's going to be tough for a while until you get accustomed to it and train people."

The consultant had a clear idea of the final form he wanted the program to take and strong beliefs regarding the best ways to accomplish the change. This single-mindedness, combined with the time constraint, probably prompted him to move too quickly through the early communication stage. Throughout the rest of the program, meanwhile, many other issues emerged. Was the consultant able to win support for the program as he headed into successive stages of the change process? Was it possible to involve employees in designing and implementing the new system? How did training figure into all this? How did changes in individual responsibilities affect support for the program?

QUESTIONS OF CREDIBILITY AND FAIRNESS

Managerial respect is tough to earn and all too easy to lose. An exaggeration here or a misrepresentation there can capsize a manager's credibility, even if that credibility has been many years in the making. This has special relevance for managers who are directing change. The process forces managers to go out on a communication limb: They must talk about what can and should be happening in the operations environment rather than what is happening. Such talk opens wide the door to credibility gaffes. Managers need to proceed with caution, realizing the implications of what they say to employees. The key is to communicate sufficiently without communicating incorrectly. This is the only way to move forward the change process while preserving the essential element of employee respect.

For consultants, the situation is a bit different and usually more difficult. Since the consultant typically is perceived as an outsider, client employees sometimes don't have a firm opinion one way or the other. The tablet is blank, so to speak, and it's up to the consultant to shape the collective opinion. The rub to all of this is that first impressions are enduring. There is little room for error, which means that respect can hinge on the first few days of face-to-face meetings with employees. Consultants also have to deal with the bias against outsiders. Employees don't want consultants meddling in their affairs, especially when the consultant has come to alter the status quo.

These issues surfaced dramatically during installation of the maintenance management program. Some employees perceived the consultant as the wrong man for the job. For example, the maintenance general foreman said the consultant was "sharp as a tack" and had thorough knowledge of the technical requirements of the program. Beyond this, however, the consultant seemed unable to generate commitment. The general foreman explained:

> Reynolds has independent-type people who know their job. When you start a program of that size, and it's going to have that kind of impact on the total maintenance product like that one did, you need a very strong man to pull it off. I think we probably would have gotten further along if we had somebody who was really strong in working with working people.

Several employees, noting the strong union presence at the plant, said the change process could have been hastened if the consultant had more experience working with unions. One maintenance employee even suggested bringing in a union member or someone who had extensive experience in operations that involve many unions. Employees at the Reynolds plant are represented by 13 different unions.

The credibility question is sometimes accompanied by a fairness question: Is the outsider going to implement a fair program? At Cleveland Electric Illuminating Co., fairness was continually stressed and ended up working to the company's advantage. Workers seemed more open to the change because it was led by former meter-readers. The management team constantly emphasized that routes were being redistricted fairly, with short ones lengthened and long ones reduced.

At Reynolds, employees were told that the maintenance management program would not reduce head count. Yet fears were never completely put to rest. "I believe they got to the point where they didn't feel he (the consultant) would be a threat to them," the maintenance general foreman said. "But I don't believe they ever got to the point where you could say they trusted him." He continued:

> You've got to get in there and let people know you want to be one of them. You don't want to be above, you don't want to be below, you just want to be their equal. If they believe you feel that way, you won't have any problems. They'll go out of their way to help you.

From his perspective at the company headquarters, VP Brown understands the skepticism that comes with bringing outsiders like consultants into the operations environment. He explained: "In industry—not just in maintenance but in accounting, administration, wherever—you'll find people who say, 'Here comes the consultant, here comes another program, and they come and go.'" The statement is true in that employees sometimes dismiss changes that don't come completely from within. However, with a change as sweeping as the installation of a maintenance management system, employees realize that the program can remain in place long after the consultant's departure. This adds a negative tone to their skepticism and can lead employees to believe the changes are even less fair.

One very tangible element of the maintenance management program is the Time Distribution Card. The card is used to record the amount of time that maintenance craftsmen spend on specific jobs, in-plant travel, rest periods, and delays. The information is necessary to generate data on operational effectiveness. Some maintenance craftsmen see it differently, believing the cards are used to monitor the performances of individual craftsmen. According to one craftsman, the cards were introduced early in the program with little explanation. "Supervision more or less brought it out and said, 'This is the way it is.'"

Five years later, the cards remain a source of resentment. Some maintenance workers quietly fight back by taking short-cuts in filling them out. Simple though they may be, the cards have become something of a symbol to maintenance workers. They provide a daily reminder of the change that was presented to them and the fairness issue that was never fully resolved during the consultant's time at the plant.

THE LIMITS OF INVOLVEMENT

Early into the project, the consultant set up an implementation team consisting of the plant manager, production and maintenance supervisors, and maintenance job planners. The team met regularly, reviewing the program during its development stages and working to resolve problems as they arose. Guiding the group was a special book designed for the maintenance management steering committee. The book provided detailed information about the new system.

The steering committee remained the main source of employee involvement throughout implementation. For better or for worse, employees at other levels never played a significant role in shaping the program. The extent of involvement was constrained because most employees had limited understanding of the planning and scheduling that goes into a structured maintenance program. Training became the area in which the consultant and employees worked together most closely.

Even though the training effort was fairly extensive, five years later, most people say the lessons didn't fully prepare them for their new responsibilities. For instance, one production employee pointed out that supervisors were given information on how to write work orders. Yet later in the conversation, the same employee cited work orders as a weak spot in the training. These criticisms would probably surface in any major change involving technical and cultural components. Training is an easy target for people who harbor discontent with the new program. What's more, the sweeping nature of the change made it nearly impossible to educate all employees successfully over such a brief implementation time. There simply was too much to be learned by too many employees.

There were gaps in the training, however, that are not easy to defend. For instance, maintenance craftsmen had little instruction on how their jobs would change and what they would have to do differently. One maintenance planner used the Time Distribution Card as an illustration.

> If you're not real familiar with some procedure, you're hesitant to do it. In training, you've got to go into detail with them (the maintenance craftsmen) so they understand the system. A 30-minute session on filling out a TDC card is not proper indoctrination. That is not training on a planning and scheduling system.

People at all levels seem to agree. Ogborne, now the plant manager, said he believes training was adequate for some personnel. But the training didn't include others whose work would affect the success of the change process. Although the time constraint and the number of employees prevented in-depth education for everyone, there probably should have been greater effort to spread the training not only to craftsmen, but also to others who would be working with the new system. Ogborne explained:

> I guess the one thing we probably should have done—and this happens with any change effort—is we should have spent a great deal more time training people. And I'm talking about all kinds of people—not just the people selected to be planners, not just the maintenance supervisors. We really didn't get production supervisors involved enough until well after the fact. We made an effort to do that, to train them, and we did some other things where they had seminars with maintenance people to understand the thing better. The training aspect is really the biggest factor, I think. When you get that many people involved in the process and you devote that time, it's money well spent.

It's less clear whether deeper employee involvement—involvement beyond training, that is—would have neutralized some of the resistance early into implementation. Recall, for instance, that few people in the plant fully understood the concepts behind a system of planned maintenance. Heavily involving those people could have proven counter-productive, especially in the short term. Furthermore, maintenance and production employees appeared comfortable with the cultural norm of spur-of-the-moment repair work. The new system called for replacement of this norm with a methodical approach based on careful planning and scheduling. It's questionable whether employees holding onto the old set of norms and values could effectively develop the technical skills required to support the new culture.

These realities made it tough going for the change managers. Ogborne described the lack of managerial options that often characterize cultural and technical change:

> No matter how you handle it, it's going to be perceived as thrust upon them because it's not something they designed, evolved, whatever. It's something they inherited. With most of these programs, if management doesn't decide that that's the way it's going to be, it never will be. If they (workers) have an option not to change, they won't change. In things like this, where there is so much money spent on the conversion and the work, you can't leave it to their discretion.
>
> A better way to sell it, of course, is to have more involvement, more training, more explanation, more conversion of their ideas into the working format of the program. Those kinds of things are what sell it. We have had an opportunity to do some things in this plant along those lines, where we've gotten the folks involved in the beginning, let them work on it very deeply, like the automation of the hot line. They were very, very involved in that. This was on such a large scale, I'm not sure we could have done that.
>
> I guess the question is, how expedient do you have to be? If we had our choice, we probably would have had more of a cross-section of people involved in the installation. I'm talking about not only salaried people, but also hourly people.

The technical aspects of the program are now fully implemented, but the change process continues. Meanwhile, greater involvement has been worked into the system. For instance, meetings are held to discuss the program and its remaining problem areas. "They come out of it with some solutions to problems we've had," Ogborne said. These contributions help chip away what remains of the old culture while adding shape to the new culture.

WORK-ETHIC IMPLICATIONS

The new maintenance management program significantly changed the nature of the maintenance craftsman's job. The craftsmen no longer have so much leeway in deciding which jobs to do and how to do them. Now, they have job plans (written by the job planners) and rigid schedules (developed by the supervisors). Hot-line employees are quick to point out that this change affected the craftsmen's attitudes and feelings toward their jobs. The craftsmen perceived that some of their control was being pulled away, and it came as a slap in the face to their professionalism. The program did not include any steps to resolve this problem or even deal with it, practically guaranteeing the presence of long-term resentment.

One foreman described the situation this way:

> The program has totally removed individual effort. In the past, we had dedicated people (that is, people who were assigned to certain areas). These people were the best. They took care of it, if you will. With the new program, that doesn't work. The new program is far more efficient, probably in utilizing manhours. But now, a mechanic is assigned a job. He does that job and he leaves. He does nothing else. If five feet away there is something that is falling apart, if there's nothing on his piece of paper he doesn't do it.

Craftsmen aren't the only ones who believe that the new program scales back the daily challenge to their work abilities. One planner explained how his job now seems more clerical than technical. The perception troubled him, yet he could think of no way to improve the situation. The maintenance general foreman belonged to the first group of planners. Reflecting on the nature of the planning job, he said:

> When I started in planning, I thought I'd have more

> control. I had been a supervisor for years. But I found myself in a situation where you're just making suggestions: Here's what we need to do, here's how many people you need. The guy on the line would say, "Forget it, here's what I really need. Don't come here telling me that we now need two people when two months ago we needed four people."

CONCLUSION

It should come as no surprise that many hot-line employees are critical of the new maintenance management system. The system called for significant cultural and technical changes, all at an operation that had remained remarkably unchanged for more than 40 years. As for measuring the success of the program, it is yielding benefits, and the benefits are being acknowledged by employees. Most employees, despite all their criticisms, affirmed the wisdom of the program by pointing to some sort of improvement. They all seemed willing to continue forging ahead with the change, implying that much of the initial uncertainty no longer exists.

The context in which the change occurred probably could not have been more challenging. Extreme unionization, coupled with the sheer complexity of the operation, made it difficult for the consultant to get off to a quick start in developing and implementing the program. Fears of job security proved especially troublesome, injecting feelings of mistrust and undermining any hope of immediate worker commitment. Also, when the program was introduced, employees were not fully told what the benefits would be. They could not form a clear sense of where the program would take them, and this heightened uncertainty. An aggravating factor involved expectations, which seemed to be set too high during the early phases of communication.

Credibility and fairness issues also surfaced. Most employees regarded the consultant, who filled the primary role of change manager, as an outsider. The perception had a negative connotation in the tight-knit work force. The consultant, they acknowledged, had the smarts necessary to implement the program, but he never became a persuasive force capable of implementing the complex program. Some workers simply felt that the consultant lacked the character traits needed to sell the program. Others regarded him as too aloof. These perceptions gave way to questions of fairness.

Involving employees in developing the program obviously had its limits because few people understood the program's components. Training partially closed the understanding gap and gave employees tangible proof that they were being involved. This was a practical way to deal with uncertainty. As for the evolution of involvement, employees are now playing a much bigger role in making technical decisions and solving problems.

A final issue involved the nature of individual jobs and how they were affected by the change. Some employees thought the maintenance management program had reduced the challenge inherent in their work roles. This seemed to wear away some of the pride they once had for their jobs and tended to make them more critical of the new system.

PART III

Now that you're equipped with three detailed examples of change management in the operations setting and have background on many other examples cited in the first chapter, we can begin building a set of practical managerial strategies and tactics.

Chapter 6 achieves this in an evolutionary sort of way. The chapter first identifies issues and concepts that characterize the operations setting. These issues are then converted into managerial strategies, which are broad guidelines for managing change. The final, and most useful, result is the managerial tactics. An agenda of tactics is provided for each strategy, giving you clear and detailed directives.

In Chapter 7, you'll go beyond knowing *what* to do. The chapter shows *how* to apply your knowledge in specific change-management situations.

The chapter begins by showing how you can accurately define the nature of the change: Is it primarily technical or cultural, or a combination? Next, you will learn how to identify issues relevant to your operation. From this, you can isolate the strategies that must be a part of the change process. The chapter also explains how to select the appropriate tactics and how to use the theoretical framework (from Chapter 2) to develop a change-management timetable. All the information is brought together in a final return trip to Starmark Manufacturing Co.

6

ISSUES, STRATEGIES, AND TACTICS

A nutshell understanding of operations is essential in developing a method for managing change in the operations environment. Tactics are based on strategies, and strategies must be based on some understanding of the current situation. With a faulty assessment of the current situation, tactics will likely have little managerial effectiveness. On the other hand, if the situation is accurately described, powerful strategies (and related tactics) should emerge quite easily.

For change managers in the operations department, the best way to assess the "current situation" is by identifying core operations issues. This requires observation, exploration, analysis, and judgment. It also requires a bit of generalizing and, yes, some stereotyping. Brevity is important. If we were to draft 10 or 20 statements describing "operations," distilling these into a workable number of change-management strategies would be impossible. Managers would face strategy overload and probably dismiss the approach as impractical. The following method steers clear of this, providing results that are thorough and practical.

Pulling together all we have covered about managing change, five core issues emerge. These issues are prevalent in the operations setting—they characterize operations—and have a direct bearing on any effort to manage change. If anything in this book deserves to be emphasized, it is these five issues: predictability, unity, pride, isolation, and fairness.

PREDICTABILITY

Perhaps more than any other functional area, operations gives its workers a sense of stability. Most operations employees have clearly defined roles they have mastered through many years of experience. At CEI, the meter-reading system remained in place for 25 years. At the company acquired by Nucor, top-down management and its operational implications had been the employee way of life for 18 years.

The extreme example of predictability in operations is the assembly-line environment. The worker carries out a single task, becoming a master of one small piece of the operation. Management literature now warns against this, and many managers have rebelled against industry's historic obsession with efficiency. But the fact is, assembly lines remain a major feature of many manufacturing and service operations.

According to some observers, automation marks the beginning of the end of the "predictable" environment. Yet in many cases, automation simply pulls predictability into the next century. Operations has a new state-of-the-art look, due in large part to automation, and jobs have changed. Relatively unchanged, however, is the repetitiveness characterizing many operations jobs. In some cases, automation has even intensified predictability by reducing the need for human judgment calls. It's all being handled by sophisticated equipment.

Admittedly, some operations jobs have a measure of variability. First-line supervisors, for instance, typically are required to wear many hats. They are involved in scheduling, planning, special projects, worker development, and other areas. But even these positions have a higher level of predictability than positions in other functional areas. The "hats" the supervisor wears throughout the day are clearly defined. Working with the same group of people over a long period of time reinforces predictability.

Some people are comfortable with the constancy this brings. They don't want surprises, and in some cases, they don't want to be challenged. Others find their jobs to be monotonous. They loathe the unchanging nature of their work and complain incessantly. Yet nearly all people, even those who drone on about their "boring jobs," grow accustomed to the sense of security that comes from knowing what to expect at the start of each working day. Change, when it comes, breaks the cycle of predictability. It takes direct aim at the security inherent in an unchanging operations environment.

Change challenges employees on any number of counts. They may have to learn new procedures, new techniques, and new machines. They may have to adjust to new personalities and new positions of authority. They even may face layoffs. So many question marks pop up, it's no wonder employees resist a break in predictability. The same work, day after day, may not be appealing, but it can look very good indeed when change suddenly threatens employees' perceived security.

Predictability doesn't relate exclusively to technical matters like equipment and procedures. Employees also can find security in a company's culture, especially when norms and values evolve at a glacial pace. AT&T is a classic example of a company that experienced a sudden disruption in cultural predictability. Since the early 1900s, the organization's culture had been moving forward slowly, sheltered by a regulated environment. Then came deregulation, with its earth-shaking competitive implications. The company had no choice but to undertake internal change in response to external change.

At the AT&T of the late 1970s, employees were accustomed to a consumer-service focus, lifetime career security, promote-from-within succession, and consensus management. Deregulation sparked the corporate equivalent of a cultural revolution. The company became market-focused. Entrepreneurship emerged as a key employee attribute, to be used in the promotion process. Units were downsized, and decentralization affected the entire organization. For employees, the new AT&T required not only the development of new work methods and behaviors, but also a change in operating norms and values.[1]

UNITY

Organized labor is the most obvious form of unity. Unionization may be on the wane in some industries, but no operations manager can ignore the fact that about 20 million Americans belong to unions. Most of these unionized personnel work in operations.

Consider that at least 75% of all U.S. workers in the transportation, contract construction, and mining industries are unionized.

The level is 50% to 74% in the primary-metals industry, the paper industry, and tobacco manufacturing. Many more industries fall into the 25% to 49% category, including telecommunications, petroleum refining, fabricated metals, lumber, and utilities.[2] Numbers like these make clear that unions remain a strong force in the work place—a force that must be reckoned with.

All of this has important managerial implications. The worst-case scenario is an "us against them" mentality. The organization splits into sharply delineated groups of managers and workers, and common ground begins to shrink. Actions are taken to benefit one side or the other, or to harm one side or the other. In the typical unionized environment, the split is not so severe, but management and workers still fall into two distinct camps. They rely on formal procedures for hammering out decisions that are perceived to be mutually beneficial.

In many change-management situations, unions can play a powerful role. A case in point is the hot line department at the Alloys Sheet & Plate Plant, where several union members raised doubts about the entire maintenance management program. Unions also played a role in the change at CEI. There, despite early warnings by union leaders that they would launch a barrage of grievances to retaliate against change, union input probably helped generate commitment among workers. No grievances surfaced. At Nucor, CEO Kenneth Iverson minces no words when discussing the unity issue as it applies to unions. If General Bearing had been staffed by a unionized work force, he says, Nucor would not have acquired it.

In some cases, the gulf between union and management seems to be shrinking. Since the 1970s, cooperation has shown up in the form of productivity gainsharing plans, labor-management committees, and quality-of-work-life projects. These efforts zero in on mutual management and union goals, involving people at all levels of the organization to make the goals attainable.[3] Operations managers, especially those who see a future need to manage change, need to monitor these developments. The rapid evolution of union-management relations offers unique opportunities to marshal support for operations change.

While unity is most obvious in the union setting, there's another form that typically is less formal yet potentially much stronger. You'll have trouble finding it in any stack of statistics, but it's hard to miss on most operations floors. This is the unity that develops when people work side by side for many years. The benefits of seniority are a motivator in keeping people in the same environment. Employees have "put in their time," and now they're reaping the benefits. They know their colleagues. There's often a family atmosphere. What's more, a promotion in operations usually finds an employee staying under the same roof. In contrast, a promotion in other functional areas often means a move to another city or state.

A manager cannot fully describe the ingredients of such unity, let alone measure it, while directing a change effort. Yet no manager can afford to ignore it. Nothing will prompt unity more quickly than an external threat. Change, perceived as a threat to predictability, will bond employees into a solid wall of resistance. At that point, management faces two equally unpleasant options: Expend tremendous energy trying to destroy the wall, or wait many years for the wall to crumble on its own. The preferred course of action, of course, is to neutralize the perceived threat early into the change process. This will allow management to deal with resistance before it starts to build. Ideally, unity should be used in a positive way. Portraying the change as a way to achieve common goals, for example, will help turn unity into a positive force that drives forward the change.

More than any other issue characterizing operations, unity has special relevance to the consultant-client relationship. At the Reynolds hot mill in Alabama, operations employees seemed dubious of "outsiders" who purported to bring improved management methods. They weighed heavily the consultant's every word. The example is anything but unique. Wherever consultants travel—wherever they are perceived as outsiders—they are likely to encounter a strengthened form of unity.

PRIDE

Like unity, pride is nebulous. It cannot be precisely defined, and it cannot be quantified. Because of this, the concept has been neglected in most management and nearly all operations literature. But failing to recognize pride can blind managers to an important force at work in many operations departments. By acknowledging this force, analyzing it, and blending it into the change process, managers can gain control of an important engine of change.

Skeptical managers can prove the force of pride by imagining a simple test: Issue to operations employees a directive that has a condescending tone or explains in agonizing detail a procedure the employees already know. What would happen? Most likely, employees would respond by somehow affirming their professional abilities. Some would seek additional work to show their worth. Some would complain directly to supervisors, or ignore the stated procedures and do things their own way. Still others would remain quietly bitter about the low regard their manager seems to have for them. Very few employees would let the directive go without some response.

At the Reynolds hot mill, many workers spoke about the pride they had in their work. Some complained that the new system extracted much of the challenge from their jobs. Recall, for instance, the maintenance job planner who said the new maintenance management system removed some of the technical aspects of his job and replaced them with clerical duties. At CEI, meter-readers also reflected a clear sense of pride. One meter-reader observed: "Not every day is going to be a good day. If every day you had a good day, it wouldn't be work. Some days you have easy days, some days you have hard days. That makes it challenging."

Managers can only speculate why this sense of pride is a trademark of so many operations settings. Psychologists may contend that people have a deeply rooted need to accomplish work, and that they personally identify with this work. Others will call it a matter of selfishness: People "own" a piece of the operation, and they don't want their control to be compromised. These explanations tie in with predictability and unity. Pride can be fueled by tangible factors like seniority and the fact that many operations employees spend a good part of their careers under one roof.

In any discussion of pride, it is requisite to raise the issue of foreign competition. Business magazines have filled thousands of pages with glowing reports about overseas operations while questioning whether American workers are equally capable or inspired. Some of the criticism, as it pertains to specific companies, is well-deserved. Every operations manager has witnessed a department or worked with a person who rates a zero on the pride scale. Yet all the research backing up this book suggests that pride thrives in many operations environments.

If anything, pride has been overridden by flawed managerial decision-making. It wasn't the auto workers, after all, who decided to stick with big cars while Japanese firms began producing downsized models. It's inaccurate to say the U.S. auto industry took a beating because workers had no professional pride. Now, with better decisions apparently being made in Detroit's board rooms, industry leaders are capitalizing on worker pride to make a worldwide comeback. Recall the ad campaign (there were several, actually) that boldly announced, "The pride is back." In fact, pride never disappeared. It was ever present, lying beneath the surface, waiting to be tapped. Now, finally, management seems to be reaching this important source of competitive energy.

ISOLATION

The terms "white collar" and "blue collar" suggest the isolation that often characterizes operations. "Management" and "worker" also show the division. This isn't just a semantic distinction with little real impact on employees. Many companies consider operations a functional area best kept separate from the rest of the organization. Often, there's even a physical separation, which means corporate staffers seldom see the products being manufactured or the services being processed. Most important, there's a philosophical gulf: Operations is thought of as an entity unto itself, as though it were its own company. This means operations is often cut out of non-operations decisions. In the same way, operations often excludes other departments when making its decisions.

For example, at most big banks, the "back office" is the operations nerve center. This is where checks are received and processed, paperwork for new accounts is completed, credit-card applications are reviewed, and so forth. The operation is never seen by customers, and it's seldom seen by employees who interface directly with customers. The story is the same, or worse, at other service and manufacturing firms. Operations workers seldom meet with customers. Sometimes, they operate in a functional vacuum, cut off from other departments.

With isolation comes misunderstanding. At too many organizations, operations is stereotyped as the "technical area"—home of the company's "dirty work," "grunt work," "boring work." The negative labels abound. This perception affects corporate decision-making and strategy development. Because operations is perceived as a technical area, many of its managers are not consulted when nontechnical decisions need to be made. Marketing executives pondering a question regarding market segmentation may not deem it necessary to consult an operations manager.

Obviously, operations doesn't have to be present and accounted for on all corporate decisions. But like it or not, nontechnical decisions often have significant implications for operations. For example, a segmentation strategy may require additional production of a certain item. Meeting this strategic goal may be possible only by boosting inventory control and beefing up the line. All of these are operations concerns. And what about operations? Yes, operations managers also are guilty of making decisions without consulting beyond departmental boundaries. The left hand has little or no idea what the right hand is doing.

The isolation problem often plagues the connection between MIS and operations when these departments are classified as separate functional areas. In developing systems to support manufacturing or service environments, MIS sometimes doesn't fully understand the operation's needs. This can result in systems that lack necessary functions or perform unneeded functions. Other times, MIS may understand the operation's support needs but have its own ideas regarding how to fill those needs most effectively. These ideas may be inappropriate given the specific constraints and conditions of an operation.

For instance, in an operation where employees will be using computers for the first time, a system that assumes high levels of computer literacy will be difficult to implement. Operations managers must ensure that MIS has inside-out knowledge of the operations environment. If operations doesn't explain in full all constraints, conditions, and objectives, MIS should collect this information on its own. MIS then must work this understanding into the system. Unless these steps are taken, the isolation factor will override the potential benefits of the change.

In the ideal situation, companies operate as a single force, with both hands working in a coordinated way. This requires management to reduce isolation as much as possible. Sound impossible? Not at Nucor, where corporate headquarters delegates considerable responsibility to the divisions. Recall, for instance, that Nucor's divisional general managers are their own personnel directors. They also are their own marketing chiefs. The general managers, in turn, delegate an impressive chunk of authority to the first-line supervisors. And the supervisors juggle all sorts of duties, only some of which fit within traditional operations boundaries. A lean corporate staff makes this not only possible but necessary. As for results, well, anyone who has kept an eye on Nucor's perennial success knows how effective an isolation-free company can be.

FAIRNESS

Fair treatment is a powerful issue in organizations of all types and sizes. As consumers, when we buy a car, we expect to get what we pay for. If we pay a below-average price, we expect basic transportation. If we pay $30,000, we expect top quality. Employees have a similar fairness rule. A fair day's work deserves a fair day's pay. Our professional sensibilities are shaken if we are unfairly compensated. There's a sense the fairness scales are off balance.

Like most of the other issues discussed up to this point, fairness can't be strictly defined or measured. Yet it must be addressed during any change process. In operations in particular, fairness takes on added meaning because of the historical overtones. The history of American manufacturing is riddled with breaches of fairness, ranging from the sweat-shop conditions that tainted the Industrial Revolution to the frightening abuses portrayed in Upton Sinclair's all-too-accurate *The Jungle*. Legislation has made the tragic extremes a thing of the past, but the legacy is too strong to be ignored entirely. Even today, many operations workers remain on constant guard against unfair treatment. And in case they ever forget about the harsh legacy of the past, parents and grandparents are quick to remind them.

Unions are the formal fairness watchdogs. Their main objective is job security, but beyond that, they also keep watch over work rules, working conditions, wages, and many other concerns. Any kind of internal change will be scrutinized. If the union perceives that the change puts workers at a fairness disadvantage, union members can be counted on to oppose it. Strikes get the most press, but they are the response of last resort. There are countless other ways that unions show their opposition. At the Reynolds hot line, the union didn't fight the change formally, but it did plant seeds of dissent among workers. Even if a change appears not to threaten the fairness balance, union anxiety can be enough to trigger opposition.

Employees in non-union organizations have been equally vigorous in fending off perceived breaches of fairness. Recall what happened at Nucor Machined Products. A profit-sharing program set up by the previous owners created an obstacle to change; some employees wanted all bonus dollars paid out before they would commit themselves to the new culture. Payment became a matter of fairness—a rallying point for some employees who wanted a sign of good faith from the new owners.

CHANGE-MANAGEMENT STRATEGIES

Each core issue described above requires a corresponding change-management strategy. These are summarized in Exhibit 6A. The strategies are general guidelines for making sure the issues work in your favor. Tactics, outlined at the end of this chapter, provide a much higher level of detail. They are the specific action steps you can take to flush out the strategies.

(PREDICTABILITY)
STRATEGY #1 — REDUCE UNCERTAINTY

Predictability reflects the stability inherent in many operations environments. Change injects a measure of uncertainty—often a significant measure—and produces an unwieldy state of perceived or actual instability. To minimize the resistance to change that's sure to arise, managers must take active steps to reduce uncertainty. They must anticipate and answer all questions and concerns that surface early in the change process. Operations employees should know with certainty what the change will bring—and when. Specific tactics to accomplish this can include meetings, memos, opportunities to "show" the results of the change, training sessions, and seminars.

Some managers tend to ignore the predictability issue. Having spent much of their time in a role that requires considerable adaptability, they often assume workers are more flexible than they actually are. As a result, managers may fail to recognize the uncertainty that change creates and the fear that results. As the change gets underway, resistance takes root. When management begins implementation, workers begin to feel their environment becoming even more unpredictable. Resistance starts to grow. All the while, management may be blinded by its assumptions, unaware of the strengthening opposition. Even a half-hearted effort to reduce uncertainty can leave room for considerable resistance. Workers do not want unknowns. Nor do they want half-knowns or contradictions. They want the facts completely spelled out because they are accustomed to a predictable environment where uncertainty simply does not exist.

The manager who actively and thoroughly reduces uncertainty should not expect this to neutralize all resistance. Some people are obsessive about predictability and will perceive any change, even one in which every phase is fully described, as unacceptable. The manager may be able to reach these people through other strategies, such as Strategy #3, Issue a Challenge.

EXHIBIT 6A

ISSUES ⇨	STRATEGIES
Predictability	Reduce Uncertainty
Unity	Secure a Commitment
Pride	Issue a Challenge
Isolation	Forge a Single Agenda
Fairness	Implement Fairness

(UNITY)
STRATEGY #2 — SECURE A COMMITMENT

Reducing uncertainty usually does not win support for change; it simply lessens resistance. To foster support, management must use tactics to secure a commitment to the change. This requires management to turn unity into a strength instead of allowing it to be a drag on the change process. An adept manager using the right tactics can create a bandwagon effect in which operations employees enthusiastically climb aboard the program.

Some of the tactics relate to involvement. If workers can be integrated into the change process, helping determine what form the change will take, they may unify in support of the change. At CEI, some workers from the bargaining unit played a role in implementation. By investing their own time in the change, they made a commitment to it. Another important tactic involves showing workers that top management is fully committed. Training also can be used to solidify commitment.

In other cases, securing commitment requires identifying and gaining the support of key people. Every organization has its natural leaders who can influence a good number of their colleagues. Formal union structures often make it easy to identify these people. It's more difficult to spot influential players in less formal employee groups, but seeking them out is well worth the effort. A public nod of approval from the right operations employee can have tremendous positive effect.

Indeed, many tactics can promote commitment. Properly fostered and guided, the right mix can be a powerful force in driving forward the change process. Rockwell International Corp., for example, has endeavored to cut away managerial layers while increasing the involvement of all employees in day-to-day operations. The effort is part of a sweeping attempt to make the company competitively solid far into the future. It has required significant change.

Commitment is the main engine driving cultural change at Rockwell's manufacturing plants. As one top Rockwell executive described: "The distinguishing feature of these (new) organizations is that high commitment by employees is presumed in the basic design of the organization. The organization is designed to generate high commitment, to fully utilize high commitment for gains, and to depend upon high commitment for its effectiveness."[4] Top management's high-level, high-visibility commitment to this philosophy seems to have bolstered individual-level commitment on the operations floor.

(PRIDE)
STRATEGY #3 — ISSUE A CHALLENGE

All the research for this book supports the fact that operations employees bring considerable pride to the work place. Managers can capitalize on this by framing the change in a way that appeals to this collective sense of pride. The most practical approach is to present a challenge and then give employees a reason for wanting to adopt the change. Properly executed, this can effectively motivate operations personnel.

Because pride is a slippery concept—we know it when we see it, but it's difficult to define and even more difficult to create—the change process is seldom presented in the form of a challenge. Specific tactics are available, however, for putting a "pride" spin on the change plan. Nucor provides one example. Its bonus program challenged workers at the company's newly purchased bearing plant to reverse course and adopt a bottom-up management system. At other companies, managers simply post notices of group performances, and worker pride prompts a vigorous rivalry. Some companies provide information about outside competition, especially foreign competition, to fire up employees' competitive determination. Consider the "Made in the USA" advertising campaign. While the primary target audience was American consumers, you can bet the campaign's planners and financiers hoped to strike a chord of pride in American workers.

What makes harnessing the positive force of pride so difficult is that not all employees respond in the same way. While some people take great pride in their work, others seem apathetic. What's more, because pride can be difficult to fire up, many managers leave well enough alone. They see little benefit from trying to capitalize on this force, especially when they're faced with a tight schedule. Reynolds employees, for example, complained that the new system removed a good deal of the challenge they had once enjoyed in their jobs. Some felt their new responsibilities were far below their skill levels. Their comments made it sound as though the new jobs were demotions. On the organizational chart, however, not a single employee was moved to a lower position.

On a broader scale, worker pride has suffered from the march of automation. Workers begrudge the fact that automation has transformed many of their jobs into monotonous routines of button-pushing. Automation seems to constrain personal initiative, creativity, and know-how. The challenge is gone, along with the days when employees could honestly call themselves "experts" in their area of the operation. Managers in highly automated environments need to be sensitive to this issue, especially when managing a change that has implications for pride.

At Rockwell International, where commitment has been woven into the organizational overhaul, employee pride plays an important role. The new value system encourages entrepreneurship and fosters the sense that employees own a piece of the business. Risk-taking, a necessary byproduct of creativity, is accepted. In place is an incentive system that rewards not only individual business units, but also individuals.[5]

Pride is also an important driving force of the "Plant with a Future" modernization effort at Caterpillar. In the February 1986 issue of *Caterpillar Folks*, the company's employee publication, an article describes the changes and explains what they're designed to achieve. Interestingly, there's an accompanying article titled, "What two competitors are doing." Without a hint of criticism, the article describes similar efforts at Deere & Company and Komatsu. Much of the text is quoted directly from the competitors' annual reports. Subtle though it may be, the report serves to fire up workers and remind them of the competitive challenges waiting outside the factory door.

(ISOLATION)
STRATEGY #4 — FORGE A SINGLE AGENDA

When managers launch a change effort in the operations department, they often find themselves cut off from the rest of the organization. This happens, as we've seen, because operations tends to be viewed as an entity worlds apart from areas like marketing, administration, finance, and the rest of the corporate office. Yet change seldom succeeds if it occurs in a departmental vacuum. In almost every organization, departments must coordinate activities in order to operate effectively. The right hand must know what the left hand is doing.

To achieve this high level of coordination, operations managers must forge a single agenda, clarifying with all departments the detailed nature of the change. They must secure a commitment from all non-operations personnel who may have some influence on the change. The agenda can be brought into focus by memos, seminars, and other methods of information exchange. If possible, the process should involve departmental higher-ups who can then transmit information about the change to their employees.

A single agenda was not forged in the early stages of change at CEI. The management team found that middle management was neither sufficiently informed nor committed. Two of the managers had agendas that did not square with the change plan. If these individuals had been allowed to pursue their agendas aggressively, the first-line supervisors directly beneath them would have been torn between two different agendas. This would have undermined commitment, sending mixed signals to the meter-readers. Fortunately, the lead change manager responded quickly enough to avert serious damage, using persuasion and authority to pull the dissenting managers into line with the main agenda.

In all change situations, commitment is a powerful force. So is the perception of commitment. If employees believe their immediate manager is committed to a change, they are likely to take it seriously. If they also know that the manager's boss and the boss' boss fully support the change, their own attention to the change process will increase dramatically. On the other hand, if one of the managers lets it be known that his support is shaky, workers will begin questioning whether it's in their own best interest to adopt the change. The same can happen if top management does not express any position—either for or against. Employees typically interpret this lack of signals as a sign of opposition.

Forging a single agenda is tricky. It's probably the most political aspect of the change process, requiring a delicate mix of lobbying, pressuring, promising, and threatening. Change managers may find people gravitating to two opposing camps. Other times, many factions may develop, or a quiet but volatile form of underground opposition may threaten the change process. If managers understand the operations environment in terms of people, power groups, and politics in general, they will be much better equipped to forge a single agenda. The appropriate tactics can then be selected.

(FAIRNESS)
STRATEGY #5 — IMPLEMENT FAIRNESS

The issue of fairness is pervasive at all organizations. In operations, the fairness balance is delicate, and employees are on constant watch to see how management's statements and actions tip the scale. Recognizing this, some managers ask: Can fairness be addressed in the process of managing change? If so, how? What are my tactical options?

These are reasonable questions. But it may be more appropriate to ask: Can I afford *not* to address the fairness issue? Ignoring fairness is almost certain to spark opposition. If change creates an unfair situation, it will be doomed from the start. On the other hand, a change-management plan that seeks specific ways to protect and, ideally, enhance fairness is unlikely to stir opposition. Of course, there are no guarantees that these measures will increase support. But they can be expected to put employees' fairness concerns to rest.

Tactics include involving workers in developing the change, or at least advising them early on of changes that may prompt fairness questions. Another tactic is to seek out influential workers and use them to convey information about sensitive aspects of the new program.

At CEI, management presented their change effort as an "evening-out process" in which meter-reading route lengths would be equalized. The approach had persuasive fairness appeal. Efforts to computerize are often introduced in terms of fairness. Employees are told the computers will ease the paperwork burden and generally make their work lives easier. Such a fairness "spin" can be very persuasive, but management must make sure it delivers. A broken managerial promise is dangerous in any situation. When the broken promise relates to fairness, however, it almost always creates insurmountable resistance to change.

CHANGE-MANAGEMENT TACTICS

Now that the general strategies have been spelled out, we can turn to specific tactics. Tactics are nuts-and-bolts implementation techniques. By following the strategic guidelines, and accounting for factors that make your own environment and change situation unique, you can assemble the tactical mix that will add considerable control to the process of managing change.

The tactics are presented in itemized form on the following pages. As you read through them, keep in mind this list is not exhaustive. If we were to contemplate all possible work environments and change situations, listing every appropriate tactic, this book would come in a three-volume set. The tactics that are listed, however, represent a stockpile of practical techniques that can be applied directly to almost all change-management situations. For this reason, you probably will not be eliminating many of these tactics when you embark on a major change effort. You more likely will add tactics customized for the situation at hand.

This assumes, of course, that your situation requires implementation of all five change-management strategies. If you determine that fewer strategies are necessary based on your analysis of relevant issues, you'll require a smaller agenda of tactics.

Recall the grid showing three types of change: technical, cultural, and technical/cultural. This classification system has an important bearing on the tactics you will choose. For instance, in Strategy #4, Forge a Single Agenda, the tactics you would employ for managing technical change are quite different from tactics for cultural change. With technical change, the change manager needs to translate the change into nontechnical terms and communicate the information to other departments. Cultural change, by comparison, requires the manager to ensure that the culture in other departments is compatible with the new culture. The tactical lineup for Strategy #4 includes other distinctions between technical and cultural change, as do the tactics for all other strategies.

On the following pages, a "(T)" indicates the tactic is useful mainly when directing technical change. "(C)" denotes tactics appropriate for cultural change. The absence of either letter means the tactic should be used in both types of change. If you are implementing a change process involving both technical and cultural elements, examine all the suggested tactics.

ISSUE: PREDICTABILITY
STRATEGY #1: REDUCE UNCERTAINTY

TACTICS:

Conduct orientation meetings with employees at all levels. Promote these meetings as question-and-answer sessions. Avoid controlling the meeting and unloading a barrage of facts about the change. These meetings can be billed as informal discussion groups.

Actively listen to employees to gauge their early response. Provide a structured mechanism for feedback. For instance, roam the department or take an informal survey. Or, organize formal feedback sessions. Respond to questions and concerns immediately. Seek out people who seem especially negative about the change. (One possible group includes long-time veterans of the "old way.") Through discussion, analyze the reasons for their position, and respond accordingly. Don't allow negative feelings to take root. Catch them early, and deal with them swiftly and decisively.

Use memos and on-the-spot meetings to round out the communication effort and to provide "emergency" responses in the event of unexpected resistance.

Secure and publicize commitment from top management. Ideally, involve top managers in question-and-answer sessions. Solicit top managers to send memos to all employees indicating their full support for the changes.

(T) As much as possible, *show* what the change entails. If it involves a new computer system, for example, give employees access to a sample terminal and software. Let them experience the benefits and resolve many of their own technical questions.

(T) Begin training sessions with influential people at various levels of the operation. Strive to make these key people more comfortable with the components of the change. Fully respond to and assist these people to ensure that their training is successful. Be sure to supply trainees with all the necessary equipment and documentation.

(C) Provide every employee with a revised policy guide that details the structural changes involved in the cultural change. Follow up with scheduled question-and-answer sessions based on information in this guide. Depending on the size of the operation, have an open-door policy on questions regarding the new policies.

(C) Show by example what the cultural change is all about. If you're an "insider," make yourself an example, demonstrating in real life the norms and values inherent in the new culture. Example: If the change aims to create a customer-first culture, publicize your recent extraordinary effort to respond to a special order.

(C) Be patient. Cultural change usually requires more time than technical change. It calls on people to change not only what they do and how they do it, but also how they think. Do not depart from this first set of tactics too quickly.

ISSUE: UNITY
STRATEGY #2: SECURE A COMMITMENT

TACTICS:

If you're an "outsider," such as a consultant or an employee from another department, link up with influential employees. Positive relationships with these people can generate the perception that the outsider has been accepted into the group.

Demonstrate expertise. Show employees you are fully familiar with the new technical and/or cultural features and are fully confident they will succeed. Provide background information if necessary. This can be especially important for "outsiders."

If the work force is unionized, approach the leadership before they approach you. Provide full information about the change effort, showing how it will not jeopardize job security or other labor concerns. Remain honest or risk losing credibility later on. If a union does not exist, but there is a strong informal leadership structure, approach the leaders, but be careful not to isolate others who may be outside this circle. Secure from influential employees some kind of commitment. Ideally, make this commitment visible to all other employees.

Continue the full communication effort begun with Strategy #1. Also, continue to conduct structured Q-and-A sessions. Respond immediately to any doubts, questions, or concerns about the change. In the case of technical change, continue to provide opportunities for employees to experience what the change is all about.

(T) Broaden the training effort to include a majority of employees. Avoid leaving influential people out of the training circle. Do not restrict training to certain groups, even if it may appear they may be the only ones who need to know the new information.

(T) Continue to publicize commitment from top management. Again, ideally, involve top managers in question-and-answer sessions. Solicit top managers to remind all employees of their full support for the technical changes.

(C) Publicize instances in which groups of employees have revealed their active support for the new culture. Example: If the new culture highly values employee entrepreneurship and a production group has just redesigned a conveyor system, mention this in communication materials related to the change.

(C) If you are an "insider," continue to make yourself an example, demonstrating in real life the norms and values inherent in the new culture. Publicize these examples as a source of company pride.

ISSUE: PRIDE
STRATEGY #3: ISSUE A CHALLENGE

TACTICS:

Install a structured method to motivate employees to support the change. In some environments, a bonus or other compensation incentive system can be installed. In addition, or where contracts prohibit this, develop a method for distributing information on a regular basis to show improvements resulting from the change. Example: productivity reports issued weekly to all workers.

Recruit influential people to monitor improvements resulting from the change. If possible, appoint them to oversee the recognition program (explained later in this list of tactics).

Exude a good measure of visible excitement about the change. In the case of technical change, distribute newspaper clippings, journal articles, and other written items that tout the technical merits of the change. With cultural change, take similar measures to show how the norms and values of the new culture represent the leading edge in operations.

Provide conclusive evidence that the change is needed. An example relating to a parcel shipping operation: Distribute information comparing the operation's on-time delivery rate to competitors' rates. Other evidence that could be used, depending on the operation, includes comparisons of productivity, labor utilization, equipment uptime, labor costs, and so forth. Performance measurements and other comparative information should be selected based on its potential to be influenced by the specific change currently underway.

(T) Demonstrate that the change moves the operation forward in terms of technical sophistication. If possible, show specifically how the change gives the operation a technical edge over the competition. Provide a tangible to support the claim. Example: Distribute an article that describes a competitor's MIS system, showing it to be inferior to the new MIS system being installed as part of the change process.

(C) Show how the new culture is better suited for the existing competitive environment. Show how successful adoption of the culture will give the company a competitive advantage. Again, provide evidence in the form of magazine or newspaper articles, copies of speeches, competitor statistics, and industry data.

(C) Develop a formal recognition award for outstanding performance resulting from display of new norms or values. In this way, attempt to generate excitement about the change. Example: a monthly cost-cutting award at an operation attempting to make cost-consciousness a major part of the culture.

ISSUE: ISOLATION
STRATEGY #4: FORGE A SINGLE AGENDA

TACTICS:

Analyze and determine the link between operations and other functional areas. With cultural change, be sure the desired operations culture fits with the overall company culture, if the two will be different. With technical change, assess the implications the change has for nontechnical areas of the organization. In all change efforts, communicate the findings to non-operations areas, making sure they fully understand the nature of the change. Whenever possible, use direct communications such as meetings, as opposed to indirect methods such as memos. Communicate with people who have sufficient authority and who will act on the information.

Monitor all responses to the change as it unfolds, looking especially beyond the functional boundaries of operations. Also observe operations groups or levels that may not be heavily involved in implementing the change. As soon as a conflicting agenda surfaces, respond by formalizing the input through a one-on-one meeting. Use logical persuasion as a first-round response. If the conflicting agenda persists, enlist employees who support the change to add their persuasive weight. Dissenters are most likely to listen to the people with whom they work closely each day. As a last resort, call on higher-ups to pull the dissenting person or group into line.

(T) Translate the objectives of the change effort in nontechnical terms. Communicate the information to other departments. This communication is tailor-made for memos, but personal meetings allow for question-and-answer sessions. Ideally, meet in person *and* provide a written report detailing the change agenda.

ISSUE: FAIRNESS
STRATEGY #5: IMPLEMENT FAIRNESS

TACTICS:

Don't assume the change is perceived by employees as being fair. Assume they are dubious, and respond right from the start by providing indisputable evidence that fairness will be fostered throughout the change process. In all forms of communication, both direct and indirect, emphasize fairness. State it directly, as in: "Our main goal is to make sure everything is above-board, completely fair, for everyone." Also, show it. Example: If the change will even out work loads, provide data showing what those work loads will be. Take every opportunity to reinforce the fairness theme.

Stay flexible to suggestions from employees. If a dispute targets one area of the program, raising a fairness question, avoid creating the perception of being immovable. Without jeopardizing the change, give some ground, perhaps by shaping a compromise. At all times, however, make sure your commitment to the change is obvious.

Be careful not to break a promise, no matter how small. This is especially important early in the change process. Example: Workers are told they will receive a new procedures manual in one week, but it's not available until the third week. Punctual delivery on a promise made early into the change will reinforce fairness, increasing trust in the process and in the change managers.

Remain alert to fairness questions and issues likely to arise as implementation unfolds. React immediately by providing a tangible response. Example: a special memo addressing the fairness questions and providing guarantees there will be no violations. Other examples: a formal meeting with employees, a letter from top management. Fairness "skeptics" may be talking to other employees, undermining support for the change. Speak with them individually to determine the underlying reasons for their resistance. Address each of these points directly, providing tangible assurances that fairness will be preserved. While doing so, reiterate the objectives of the change.

(T) As with Strategy #2, Secure a Commitment, strategically involve employees in planning the actual change. Put them in areas where their involvement will be satisfying. However, guard against involving employees to the point of jeopardizing change outcomes. Seek out people whose involvement may have symbolic value.

(C) Involve employees in the effort to establish the new culture. An example from a company setting out to build an environment in which "the customer is king": Set up an improvement team to identify specific ways to strengthen client relations.

7

AN ACTION PLAN FOR CHANGE

The theories, examples, case studies, issues, strategies, and tactics outlined in the preceding pages supply you with considerable information about the operations change process. The key, of course, is to take the insights and *use* them to your benefit in a real change-management situation. It isn't easy, as you probably can imagine. Every effort to apply managerial recommendations is marked with pitfalls that can snare the most well-intentioned manager, and this one is no exception.

This chapter is designed to help you steer clear of the pitfalls. It offers guidance and puts a practical spin on everything you've read so far, explaining how to:

1. Identify the nature of the change.
   Is it technical or cultural, or does it involve components of both? Where is the change located when plotted on the x-y grid?

2. Analyze the operations department.
   Which issues and accompanying strategies are relevant? What unique conditions and constraints are part of the operation? What other factors shape the department? Are these likely to affect the change process?

3. Select the appropriate tactics.
   Use the agenda of tactics presented in Chapter 6. Tailor tactics to fit the specific operation and nature of change. Develop your own tactics if necessary.

4. Develop a schedule.
   This shows how the change will unfold. The theoretical material in Chapter 2 serves as a framework.

DEFINING THE CHANGE

Recall the change grid introduced at the start of Chapter 3. Simple though it may be, the grid offers a useful way to categorize specific types of change.

Although determining the grid location of a change can be tricky, managers need to make this determination with confidence in order to select the appropriate tactics. Without knowing the extent to which a change is technical or cultural, or both, selecting tactics can turn into a risky guessing game. A good first step to learning how to use the grid is to look at several examples.

EXAMPLES

In Exhibit 7A, management has plotted a change involving installation of a bar-code system to improve warehouse inventory control. Until now, inventory clerks have recorded issues and receipts using hard-copy inventory forms. The forms are entered into a computer system each week by a separate data processing department. Computer use by operations employees has been minimal.

The new bar-code system offers real-time updating of inventory records, significantly improving the accuracy and speed of the entire inventory process. The change involves many technical components: computer software and hardware, bar-code reading equipment, and labeling procedures. In addition, a procedures manual explains the new system and how it will improve inventory management. Part of the implementation will require training because warehouse clerks will work directly with the system.

Cultural impact is negligible. The norms and values of opera-

EXHIBIT 7A

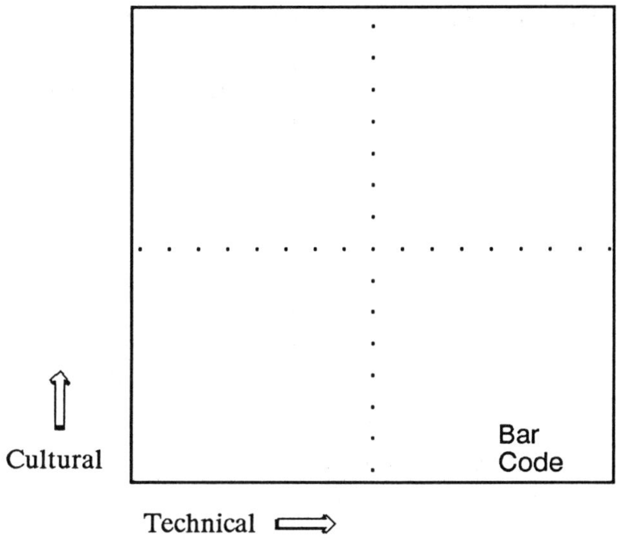

EXHIBIT 7B

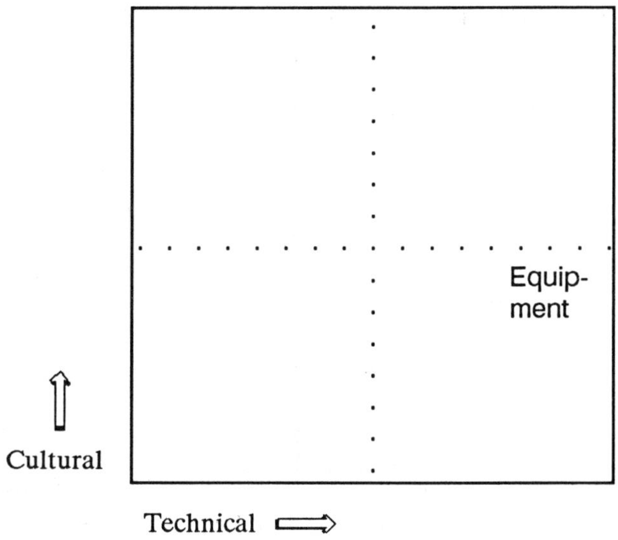

EXHIBIT 7C

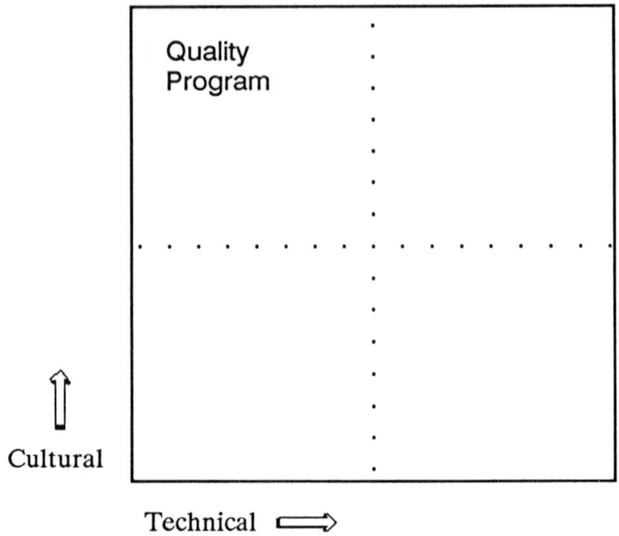

EXHIBIT 7D

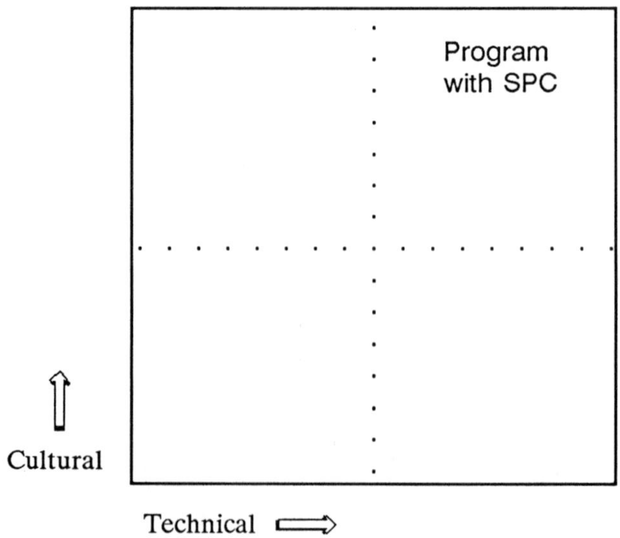

tions employees, particularly those whose jobs relate to inventory management, will not change. They are not intended to change. The fact that the system is designed to bring greater control to the inventory process may underscore in employees' minds the importance of the inventory function. But this is unlikely to change culture, intentionally or otherwise.

The next example, Exhibit 7B, depicts the installation of sophisticated equipment in a printing plant. The plant has been operating with 25-year-old equipment, and the new presses represent a significant technological advance. Considerable training will be required for all pressmen.

Quality and prompt delivery always have been valued by operations employees at this printing operation. But in recent years, these cultural trademarks have begun to weaken. Many employees have been complaining about the old equipment, saying it hampers their best efforts to meet the company's demanding quality standards and delivery dates. Some are starting to think the higher-ups have put cost control above quality. Management is confident the installation will energize the organization's culture of quality and customer service. Thus, the change process has a cultural side. However, the change is mainly technical, as shown on the grid. Managers may want to examine tactics that relate specifically to cultural change and implement some of these. But they have no pressing need to integrate these tactics into the overall change effort.

Exhibit 7C shows the grid position of a cultural change. An organization is attempting to make all operations employees more sensitive to product quality. The goal is to turn every employee into a quality manager. Specifically, the company is forming quality focus groups in which employees take on quality problems and develop improved methods. An informal incentive program will be set up to recognize outstanding work that moves the company closer to its quality objectives. Aside from learning how the quality focus groups will work, employees will have few technical issues to deal with during the change process. The company is setting out to reshape the values of the operations work force.

Exhibit 7D shows the same change as in plot C—with the addition of statistical process control (SPC) as a technical tool for boosting quality. The company wants to use SPC in order to gather objective production data. This will enable the quality groups to direct improvement efforts to where they're needed most.

Implementation of SPC will require special training because in this case, it requires not only the adoption of new technical concepts, but also the use of new measuring equipment. Much of this technical work will involve a handful of key production people, and most already have experience working with SPC. Thus, in this example, the technical slant is limited, though the change process still falls within the technical/cultural quadrant. If management decided more workers should learn about SPC, or if key production personnel knew very little about this quality-control tool, the plot would move to the right, suggesting added technical emphasis.

Yet another plot shows a different cultural/technical change. In Exhibit 7E, implementation of a just-in-time inventory system (JIT) requires adoption of a new technique *and* a change in manufacturing philosophy. In this case, the change is occurring at a high-volume producer of circuit boards. Once JIT is in place, the operation will no longer be plagued by enormous inventories and the problems involved in managing them. What's more, production will be continuous, in contrast to the stop-and-go flow that characterized the previous system.

EXHIBIT 7E

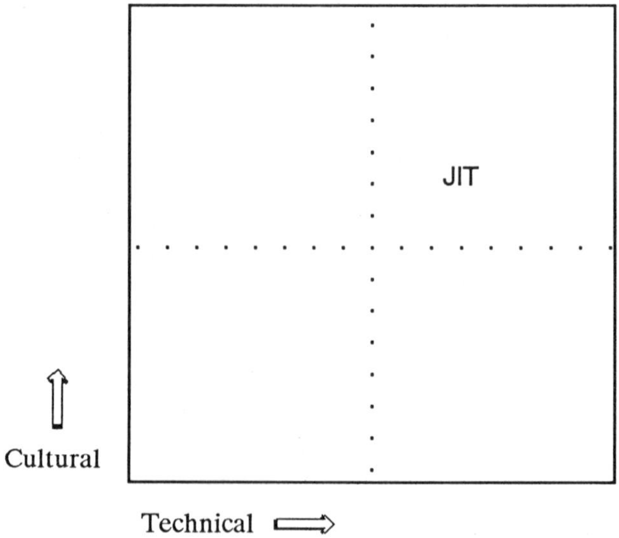

All of this will require major change in employees' attitudes and values. There will be much less room for error in all inventory calculations, since raw-material inventories will be sharply downsized. And production planners, analysts, and engineers will have to be closer to the production line. The change will be sweeping, involving technical and cultural elements.

ANALYSIS

The examples show the usefulness of the change grid: It provides controlled, objective assistance in making an important managerial judgment call. Sometimes, however, it's impossible to look at the grid and immediately identify the position of the change. When this happens, change managers must analyze the nature of the change in a formal way. Only with such information can they use the grid effectively.

Analysis can be carried out using the following questions. Your answers will automatically narrow the area in which a specific change process should be positioned on the grid. No, precise answers to these questions will not steer you to a single, well-defined position. But a thorough analysis, based on the following questions and additional observations, will remove much of the guesswork and associated risk.

> What are the current norms of the operation? After the change process unfolds, will these norms be different? If so, is this change intentional or unintentional?
>
> If the norms will not be altered, the change most likely has a technical slant. If norms change unintentionally, the change is likely technical/cultural. At the very least, it has significant cultural overtones that position the change in the northeast quadrant of the grid. If a change in norms is intentional, the change process obviously is cultural.
>
> Who will be affected by the change process? To what degree will specific positions be influenced or changed?
>
> Technical change usually involves fewer people than cultural change. Cultural change tends to be sweeping; it should be felt by everyone in the operation. But remember, this is only a rule

of thumb. Exceptions can occur, especially at companies that have highly autonomous operating units. This can give way to a divergence in culture throughout the organization.

Why is the change being implemented? How long will it take before significant improvements are realized?

Technical change often relates to improvements of specific functions in the operations department. For example, installation of a bar-code system may aim to increase the speed, accuracy, and real-time capability of inventory management. Results will be apparent as soon as the system is in place and people know how to use it.

Cultural change often has broader goals. For example, management may want to shape an environment in which customer needs are paramount. Or, they may attempt to make group initiative and creativity a prime force for stirring innovation throughout an operation. Because of the breadth of these changes, results will come gradually—certainly more slowly than in the case of technical change.

Does the change process include installation of new equipment? To what degree is this equipment different from what already is being used in the operation? Will employees have to be trained to operate it?

"Yes" to any of these questions suggests technical or technical/cultural change.

Does the change involve techniques that are new to an organization? To what degree do these qualify as highly technical approaches?

Techniques can include materials requirements planning, just-in-time inventory, statistical process control, project management, forecasting, systems developments, and so forth. All have varying levels of technical sophistication. Some require new technology. In other cases, the technique may be more of a philosophy than a rigid approach. The presence of such techniques usually suggests a technical component to the change, but not always.

If the answers to these questions still leave you unable to find the correct position on the change grid, you may want to re-examine the core reasons for the change. You also may want to evaluate the implementation plan as it currently stands. Revisiting the very genesis of the change process can reveal contradictions or a lack of coordination. The system you had in mind may not be the best way to reach your objectives. Or, your objectives may not be flushed out, making it mere guesswork to decide specific features of the change. Elements of the new system may contradict each other, setting up the operation for a counter-productive and frustrating future.

In short, if it seems very difficult to characterize the nature of the change, the change probably has not been fully thought out. Unless managers take time at this stage to revisit and rework these issues, they'll face bigger problems further into the change process. Returning to the starting point once the forces of change are moving will be much more difficult—perhaps even impossible.

IDENTIFYING RELEVANT ISSUES

It was said earlier that change managers should err on the side of too many change strategies (and accompanying tactics) if it's unclear whether one or more specific issues is relevant. This statement was made in the interest of safety. It will guarantee that all bases are covered. Such an approach, however, has an obvious downside: It can be inefficient. And it can be unrealistic when management has to move quickly. Ideally, managers should have a programmed method for identifying relevant issues.

The following list of exploratory questions serves this purpose. When embarking on an effort to implement change, the change manager should provide honest answers in order to draw a realistic portrait of the operation. No, the questions don't guarantee full objectivity, nor do they cover all that can be asked. But they do provide a thorough, methodical approach for analyzing a particular organization. Correct answers will nudge managers in the right direction when they're groping to find issues that have a bearing on their operations department.

A word of warning: While the organized nature of this approach is useful, it can afflict managers with analytical tunnel vision. Be careful not to restrict your research to the following questions, or you'll run the risk of missing important features of your operation. A second warning: Answering the following questions will allow you to see the trees, but determining whether an issue is relevant requires seeing the forest. There's no objective way to move from "tree view" to "forest view"—that is, from simply answering the following questions to deciding which issues are applicable in your change-management situation. This will require a managerial judgment call, but you can simplify that call if your analysis is thorough.

ISSUE: PREDICTABILITY

What has happened during the past 10 years at your company with respect to change? Has the operation remained remarkably constant, or has it experienced any forms of internal change? If change has occurred, how did these change processes unfold? Did the change spark resistance? If so, how did management respond?

What is the average seniority level? Is the operations department staffed by a "veteran" work force that has logged many years with the company?

Do employees perform a variety of tasks throughout the day, or are their jobs relatively unchanging?

What is the total number of operations employees? How much has this number fluctuated during the past 10 years? Have these fluctuations been matched by changes in the company's day-to-day procedures and practices?

How have specific jobs changed during the past 10 years? For instance, what changes have taken place in the role of first-line supervisor? If a supervisor from 10 years ago were placed in the same position today, could he or she still successfully perform the job? (Conduct this informal test for all positions potentially affected by the change.)

How has the organization chart evolved? Has management

shifted around the lines of authority in recent years, or has organizational structure remained relatively unchanged? Do people often change positions within the organization?

If management announced a major internal change, how would employees respond? Generally speaking, would their reaction be positive or negative? Why would they respond this way?

ISSUE: UNITY

Is the operation unionized? If so, how strong is employee support for the unions?

Are operations workers represented by more than one union? If so, how are relations between the unions? Do the unions work together to promote mutual goals?

Has the operation experienced any labor disputes during the past 25 years? If so, how did these disputes affect the sense of unity among operations workers? To what degree do these feelings exist today?

If the operation is not unionized, do employees have formal procedures for conveying their opinions to management?

Given the level of seniority at the company, has a certain camaraderie emerged among employees based on their years of working together in the operations department?

Do workers gather for social activities during off-hours?

Does management use goal-setting programs to improve quality, productivity, or other important factors? If so, are these efforts geared toward individual or group effort? Have the techniques succeeded?

Does the nature of work at the operation require employees to work in groups, or do they work individually?

Does the company make a practice of hiring employees' relatives and friends?

Does the operations work force include any natural leaders—charismatic people who are able to energize a large number of fellow employees? (This question applies to union and nonunion environments alike.)

If changes have occurred at the operation during the past 10 years, how have operations employees responded as a group?

ISSUE: PRIDE

Does the operation make use of quality circles, focus groups, or similar methods to improve productivity and quality? Do these efforts yield measurable improvements?

Does the operations work force show concern about competition? In discussions about competition in the world marketplace, how do operations employees respond?

Does the company give out achievement awards, like an Employee of the Month award? If so, how are these incentives regarded? Do operations employees take them seriously? Why or why not?

What kinds of operations data are routinely shown to operations employees? Do employees have access to productivity or quality measurements? Are they provided with expense information like cost of materials by month or quarter? How do employees respond to the availability—or lack of—such information?

To what degree do operations employees personally identify with their jobs? If management unilaterally changed certain aspects of a worker's job, how would that worker respond? What if management asked for a complete job change?

ISSUE: ISOLATION

Is the operations department physically separated from the rest of the company? What is the extent of this separation? Are operations facilities geographically detached, located in other cities or states?

How often do operations workers mingle with employees from other functional areas? If they get together often, what are the reasons?

How do employees from other functional areas generally regard the operations department? How do operations employees regard non-operations departments?

Do operations employees ever interface directly with customers? If so, how often and under what circumstances?

Do employees ever transfer from operations into other functional departments, or vice-versa?

Does the organization chart reveal a gulf between operations and other departments? (For example, the chart may show a lack of managerial connection between departments, making operations appear as though it were its own company.)

Does the operations department have its own achievement awards separate from the rest of the company, or are awards distributed on a company-wide level?

Do company-wide improvement efforts involve employees from various departments, including operations? Or are these efforts carried out on a department-by-department basis?

ISSUE: FAIRNESS

Have fairness questions surfaced at the operation during the past 10 years? What was the nature of these questions, and how were they resolved?

Who, if anyone, serves as the operation's "fairness guardian"? (This may be union leadership, a group of employees, or even an individual.) How effective is this person or group in raising concerns about matters of fairness?

How does the operations work force perceive management in terms of fairness? If employees were polled on the fairness issue, would they describe management as generally fair or unfair?

Do operations employees point to specific managers as being especially unfair? Have any events or incidents occurred to transform certain managers into symbols of unfair management practice?

SELECTING TACTICS

The stockpile of tactics presented in Chapter 6 shows many of the options available to change managers. In some cases, it's appropriate to apply all the tactics related to a particular type of change. But more often, you should be more selective, gathering only those tactical tools that will contribute directly to the change process. This is the only way to avoid getting bogged down in more tactics than the change situation requires. And it will keep you from unwittingly taking actions that may work to your disadvantage.

We already know one way to trim the number of tactical options: Identify the relevant change-management issues. For each issue that has no bearing on the operation—and, by extension, on the change process—a full set of tactics is eliminated. But let's assume our analysis reveals that three issues are relevant. This still leaves a wide range of tactical options. How does a change manager know when it's necessary to pick and choose instead of applying all available tactics? Furthermore, if it's necessary to limit the tactics, how does the manager determine which to keep and which to drop? Is there a way to avoid turning the situation into an exercise in guesswork?

Fortunately, there is, thanks to managerial constraints. Every operation is loaded with them: time constraints, personnel constraints, organizational constraints. By analyzing the limiting factors at work in your operation, you can acquire a feeling for which tactics will work and which will likely fail. In some cases, you'll recognize tactics that are sure bets for pushing forward the change process. You also will get ideas on how to tailor tactics to fit a specific operation and change effort. Other times, you'll spot tactics likely to drag down the change process.

More often, knowing the constraints does not magically lead you to the right tactics; the analysis simply points you in the right direction. Change managers should combine their understanding of constraints with their earlier analysis aimed at determining relevant issues. After adding in experience, intuition, and judgment, you'll be fully prepared to make your tactical picks.

TIME CONSTRAINTS

The time factor plays a major role in constraining operations. At Cleveland Electric Illuminating, the change managers wanted to finish restructuring the meter-reading route system before a utility-rate change took effect. They knew all too well that if their work was not finished before then, billing would be thrown into turmoil. Finessing the change into place couldn't be done given their schedule. There simply wasn't enough time for a full agenda of tactics. They adapted accordingly.

For example, meter-readers were not significantly involved in shaping the new system, though the change managers took advantage of several opportunities for high-visibility involvement. In addition, employees were not "shown" the change; they had few opportunities for testing and tinkering with the new system. Rather, the change was explained to them by field supervisors. Given the time constraint, some tactics that may have eased the change process had to be abandoned.

If you face a situation in which time is in short supply, examine each available tactic and determine the amount of change-management work time it will likely require. Compare those estimates to the schedule of target times for implementing the change, and pare down the tactical agenda as needed. Admittedly, this is a subjective exercise, but it's better than leaving the timing issue to chance. And it's the surest way to alert change managers to an overambitious approach.

PERSONNEL CONSTRAINTS

Personnel also can constrain operations and prompt the need to trim the tactical agenda. Factors include the number of personnel, their skills, their personalities, and logistics.

In some cases, there may be insufficient manpower to carry out certain tactics. A change manager may find himself having to direct the change process single-handedly. Implementation typically is left to a management team of two or three people. With only so many hours in the day, management may be forced to limit the tactical choices to those that can be reasonably supported by available personnel. In the case of a technical change, for example, it may be impossible to provide thorough training to hundreds of employees, especially if they are scattered over a wide geographic area.

A lack of certain skills also can prove to be a serious constraint. Use of some tactics requires specialized forms of expertise. Change managers themselves may not have the needed know-how, and it may be impossible to find and utilize someone who does.

Training programs are one area where unrefined skills can wreak havoc with a change process. What's to be done if training is needed but effective trainers are unavailable? Should managers throw out training altogether, or should they try to hobble through the best they can? If training is imperative, it's time to reshape the tactic to fit the constraint. One alternative is to hire trainers from outside the company. Another option is to alter the traditional training approach to accommodate the constraint—perhaps by developing a self-tutor training format. Understanding the extent of the skills constraint can help you make these decisions, whether they involve training or other tactics requiring special skills.

Employee personalities also can play a significant, although more subjective, role in constraining your change implementation. When the traditional ways of doing things are altered, personalities often emerge and take on added force. Like it or not, change is an emotional issue. Management must assess the people involved in the change, taking their personalities and likely reactions into account. This information can be used as a basis for selecting, tailoring, and eliminating certain tactics.

Consider a situation in which several key people tend to influence the thinking of their co-workers. Several tactics should be selected in an effort to build support for the change among these people. That may require training them early in the process or involving them in shaping the actual change.

Logistics also can narrow the tactical choices available to change managers. For example, the change may involve many small facilities located across a wide stretch of the country, creating a geographic constraint. This can complicate the effort to forge a single agenda, making it essential to select tactics related to agenda-building. When the change process involves international operations, managers need to address not only geographic gulfs, but also cultural differences. Certain tactics may need to be selected, and others may need to be modified.

Even if the change affects a single facility, the layout of that facility can have a significant impact. Imagine a cramped operation with no space for training and inadequate resources to communicate with employees. Unless this constraint can be eased by improving the situation, it obviously will influence the tactical choices the change managers decide to make.

When facing such logistical constraints, be careful not to buckle under and throw out tactics whose implementation may at first glance appear to be difficult. If the tactics are necessary for successful change, they can be altered to fit unique circumstances. For instance, if change involves several long-distance plant locations, a separate change manager can be stationed at each. If the change reaches overseas to an international facility, the change managers may want to have at least one veteran foreign employee on their change-management team.

ORGANIZATIONAL CONSTRAINTS

Constraints also emerge from the structure of the organization. Lines of authority, the most tangible form of structure, can determine how much influence a change manager can bring to bear on a change-management situation. They also can frustrate the well-intentioned manager more than any other constraint—perhaps because the manager cannot sidestep or easily neutralize the constraint. Frustration usually surfaces when change managers set out to select their tactics and realize their limited authority keeps them from implementing a full tactical plan. On the other hand, lines of authority sometimes work to your advantage. Your formal position and connections within the organizational structure may set you up perfectly for turning the tactics into effective action.

Change managers who face authority constraints can find themselves in a no-win situation. They are expected to manage the change process, yet they lack sufficient clout to implement some of the necessary tactics. If they try to wield too much authority, they can compromise their own standing in the organization. If they neglect important tactics, however, they can doom the change process. No easy solutions are available. The only sound approach is to analyze this constraint at the very start of the process, gauging the risks involved. It may be necessary to review the dilemma with top management, securing a level of authority that adequately supports the change process.

Another potential organizational constraint is unionization. Union contracts prohibit certain activities and policies in the operations setting, ranging from the crossing of craft lines to the use of incentive-based compensation. For instance, Nucor's bonus program would likely be much more difficult, if not impossible, to implement at unionized work places. At the same time, unionization can add importance to certain tactics. Those that relate to securing a commitment and forging a single agenda can be vital when employees are formally represented by unions. Early communication with union leadership, for example, can stave off budding resistance.

DEVELOPING A SCHEDULE

Recall the theoretical framework for managing change presented in Chapter 2. The framework consists of three steps: unfreeze, move, refreeze. These steps form the most effective way to schedule the implementation of change-management tactics.

The "unfreezing" stage lays the groundwork for the change process. Employees must be motivated to let go of their old technical and cultural approaches, and they must be prepared to accept a new approach. During the "move" stage, the operation is in transition as it adopts the change. Training, managerial commitment, and adequate resources are just a few of the issues important during this phase of the process. In the "refreeze" stage, management attempts to solidify the acceptance of the new methods. Organizations are in a constant state of flux; after any change, there are pressures to slip back to previous operating methods. Refreezing is an attempt to keep the new approach in place, warding off any temptation to slip back to the familiar ways of doing things.

This three-step framework is used to develop the broad schedule shown in Exhibit 7F. The schedule illustrates the relative

EXHIBIT 7F

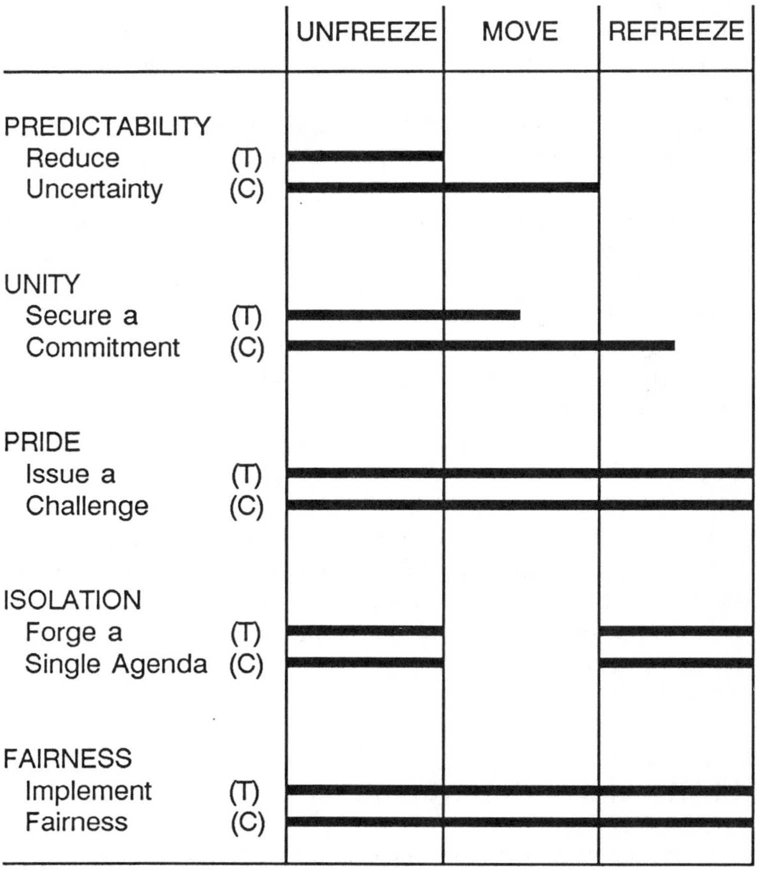

amounts of time typically necessary to implement tactics for each of the five strategies. It also shows which strategies overlap—and when. Technical and cultural change processes are distinguished, with cultural change (and technical/cultural change) emerging as the most time-consuming.

The exhibit only points you in the right direction. It does not attempt to put real time values on any of the strategies because no two change efforts are exactly alike. Different organizations may have the same objective—to implement a quality control system driven by statistical process control, for example—but constraints always differ dramatically. This yields very different time requirements for similar tactics, making it impossible to standardize the scheduling procedure with a safe degree of accuracy.

When setting out to create a detailed schedule, revisit the information you've already gathered: the nature of the change, the analysis of relevant issues, the review of all constraints. Then, using the exhibit as a guide, list the tactics in the order in which you intend to implement them. Note which tactics will unfold at the same time. Only after you've completed this step should you assign time estimates for each tactic. When unsure how much time a tactic will require, err on the side of too much time. It's much easier—and more satisfying—to move up the implementation schedule than to push things back.

The best rule is to make sure the change unfolds steadily. A glacial pace will increase the risk of sudden, unexpected pockets of resistance. A sporadic approach will confuse employees and make them question whether management is truly committed to the change. A flurry of quick maneuvers may not allow sufficient time for tactics to have an impact on all employees. Only a steady, controlled pace will assure that the tactics effectively push forward the change process.

A FINAL VISIT TO STARMARK MANUFACTURING CO.

Remember our two visits to Starmark Manufacturing? In the first version of the Starmark story, the production manager single-handedly tried to implement a just-in-time inventory system. Employees turned their back on the prospect of change, and the effort fell flat. In the second version, the manager developed strategies for each of the three change steps: unfreezing, moving, and refreezing. Implementation unfolded smoothly, but after a while, the manager sensed an undercurrent of resistance. It was growing stronger and keeping the program from reaching its potential. The manager knew he had to respond, first by pinpointing the source of the resistance, then by analyzing why the change was being pushed aside. But as he began examining the situation, he only became more frustrated. Resistance could be felt, no doubt about that. But what was the source? And why? What could be done?

If you like pat endings, you're probably not very satisfied with the way things have played out at Starmark Manufacturing. Let's take a third trip to the company, retelling the story one last time. The background information remains the same, but in this version, assume the production manager has read this book. He's familiar with the strategic approach outlined on the preceding pages and intends to use it in implementing the just-in-time inventory program.

Our story begins in a well-polished office, where the president of Starmark Manufacturing is wringing his hands over the company's inventory woes....

"We're our own worst enemy. Our levels of work-in-process and finished goods inventories are way too high. We need to seize control once and for all. Find a solution and I'll back you all the way, whatever it takes."

The production manager of Starmark Manufacturing Co. had heard these words before. Most of the words, that is. "Find a solution and I'll back you all the way, whatever it takes." That comment was a first. About time, the manager mused.

For too many years, Starmark had been plagued by excessive inventories and unpredictable delivery delays. The lack of control translated into a staggering annual expense. At least two prized customers had taken their orders elsewhere. The company president, meanwhile, balked time and again when asked to support full-scale solutions to Starmark's problems. Years passed, and the situation grew worse. Now, finally, the production manager had been handed his long-awaited mandate. He could bring to the company what it desperately needed: major change in the operations department.

During the past several years, the production manager had

carried around certain convictions. He had in mind a system that would put an end to Starmark's problems and, in the long term, boost its market position. The manager had worked with the system at another company, where he had witnessed significant benefits: reduced setup times, reduced work-in-process inventory, faster delivery. The industry called it just-in-time inventory. The production manager considered it Starmark's last and best hope for pulling production out of its costly rut.

He knew, however, that his enthusiasm alone would not lead to a successful JIT program at Starmark Manufacturing. No, it would be much more complicated. Few of the people whose jobs would be affected by the new system had ever seen JIT in action. They would be dubious, they would be anxious. They would have to be convinced.

The manager returned to his desk and jotted down the following nutshell agenda:

1. Define the change.
2. Analyze our operations department.
3. Draw up the tactical plan.
4. Draw up a schedule.
5. Implement.

DEFINING THE CHANGE

The first step seemed easy enough. The manager drew a simple four-square grid, labeling the y-axis (culture) and x-axis (technical). He then picked up a marker and put a check in the southeast quadrant. No sooner had the ink dried than he wished he had used a pencil. Conversion to a just-in-time inventory system suddenly seemed more cultural than anything else. People would have to think of inventory in a completely different way, which would mean a sharp turn in attitudes. He scratched over the original check mark and placed a second one in the northwest quadrant. But did this make sense? Introduction of a JIT program would require training. The system involved technical issues—nothing extremely difficult, but enough to qualify the change as having a slight technical slant. The second check mark went the way of the first, and a third appeared in the northeast quadrant.

The marked-up grid convinced the manager that the first stage involved more facts and less guesswork than he had anticipated. It also suggested the need for second and third opinions. He called his assistant and presented the exercise, keeping his own results under wraps. Interestingly, the assistant followed the same trial-and-error path to the northeast quadrant. His conclusion: JIT involves not only technical elements, but also cultural elements, like employees' attitudes toward on-time delivery. In the past, he noted, there wasn't all that much concern. If JIT were to survive, let alone thrive, this concern would be essential.

The production manager placed a third call, this one to the inventory control manager. An avid supporter of JIT, the inventory chief had been waiting months for the president's go-ahead. The call came more as a relief than a surprise, and he eagerly accepted the challenge to define the change. The next day, he placed a sheet of notes on the production manager's desk.

"In the left-hand column are all the cultural issues we'll have to deal with," he said. "On the right are all the technical issues we'll have to cover. I always knew it would be a tough job, but the point hit home when I wrote all this down. As for defining the change, I'm certain it falls in the northeast quadrant."

The three Starmark managers spent several hours discussing their thoughts on the matter. In the process, they positioned the JIT implementation more precisely on the change grid.

ANALYZING THE OPERATIONS DEPARTMENT

With the first step completed, the production manager returned to his note pad. This time, he began with a pencil, knowing these early exercises offered one of those rare opportunities in the change process when mistakes could be completely erased.

As a first step on what he envisioned would be a long journey, the manager wrote five words on the note pad:

predictability, unity, pride, isolation, fairness

These issues would have to be examined separately. Did each issue pertain to the Starmark operation? If so, to what degree? The manager had five lists of questions—one for each analysis. Until this study was conducted, he believed, it would be risky business indeed to begin the hands-on work of implementation.

The manager had been with the company for some time and believed he could carry out the analysis himself. But he knew that over time, he had developed a good handful of preconceptions about the way things worked at Starmark. Would these beliefs slant the study? Intent on proceeding cautiously, the manager decided to take the extra time to diversify the views. The result, he hoped, would be a more accurate portrait of the operation. The next day, he met with three colleagues who could offer the needed input.

"Our objective," he told them, "is to analyze this operation as thoroughly as possible. What forces are at work here? Where does change fit in? How are people likely to react? Part of our search will involve fairly straightforward things—like gathering turnover rates and seniority information. Other times we'll just be throwing out opinions. I'm hoping to generate a full understanding of this operation so we can truly manage, in a controlled and organized way, the implementation of JIT."

The three Starmark employees involved with the production manager in this step included his assistant, the inventory control manager, and the plant manager. Among this group, the production manager was the most familiar with the strategic approach for managing change. He was not surprised when the inventory chief asked precisely how the study would unfold.

"We'll examine five areas," the production manager responded. He named the five change-management issues and described the related strategies. "If we find that all five issues characterize our operation, we'll need to employ all five change-management strategies in implementing JIT. On the other hand, if we find that only three issues are relevant, we'll need only three strategies. Solid analysis will show what we need to include in our change effort. And it'll keep us from slipping and sliding in confusion later in the game, when it'll be much harder to turn back or change course."

During the following two weeks, working on and off together and individually, the four Starmark employees analyzed the organization. The production manager, for example, began with a list of questions.

"Has the department experienced any significant changes in the past 10 years?"

"To what degree do employees perform many different tasks

throughout the day? Are their jobs relatively unchanging?"

"What is the total number of operations employees? How has this number fluctuated during the past 10 years? Have Starmark's procedures changed over the years?"

Some questions called for simple, objective answers. Others required a good measure of subjectivity. After a while, certain themes began to emerge. Pride and unity made a strong showing, just as the manager had expected. But the analysis also offered some surprises. He met with his assistant, and they compared their findings. Again, both made unexpected discoveries about the operation.

The study concluded with a final group meeting in which the production manager worked to pull together the four different chunks of analysis. The exercise revealed definite trends and themes at Starmark that were relevant to the five change-management issues. For example, all four analysts identified pride and unity as strong features of the Starmark operation. The issue of fairness also surfaced. Two weeks earlier, the production manager recalled, he would have downplayed the issue. But the analysis had opened his eyes.

"All my research suggests workers at this company are extremely sensitive to matters of fairness," he said. His colleagues nodded in agreement.

"Remember what happened two years ago?" the plant manager said, grimacing.

He recounted the story of the production supervisor who made life miserable for several production-line veterans. The supervisor had claimed the workers were dragging down his reputation by lagging on the job. To management's discredit, no one above the supervisory level seemed to notice. Employees concluded that management was intentionally looking the other way while letting the supervisor whip a few laggards into shape. Management eventually realized what was happening and turned its sights on the supervisor. But the damage had been done. Even today, the fairness issue remained a source of tension, largely because of memories of the overbearing supervisor.

Isolation emerged as another surprise issue. The production manager always knew the operations department led a fairly solitary life, but not until now did he realize just how autonomous things had become. At one time in Starmark's history, corporate headquarters was stationed in an adjacent building. But five years ago, corporate moved to the city's business district, and the communications link between plant and office seemed to suffer.

"Remember the old days when we'd have those group meetings?" the plant manager asked.

The inventory chief interrupted: "The old days? Heck, that was just five years ago."

"You're right," the plant manager said. "It seems far off, though, doesn't it? Except for our quarterly meetings, when was the last time operations really sat down with finance, marketing, and the rest of corporate? You just don't see that happening."

The production manager chuckled. "Whenever I'm in the mood for a surprise, I just call the folks downtown. They're always up to something I'm not aware of."

When analyzing predictability, the group identified several contradictions. On the one hand, the operation seemed to be a constant for many employees with considerable seniority. Yet the production manager had begun hiring younger workers who seemed much less willing to follow old-time methods. Also, although many lines on the organization chart had remained cemented in place for 10 years, a new quality group had been added to the chart, representing perhaps the biggest change in recent memory. On the whole, however, the operation had remained remarkably predictable during the past quarter century. Starmark was a safe haven for people who wanted to punch in and punch out. For better or for worse, employees approached each shift with the confidence that no nasty surprises awaited them.

By the end of the meeting, all four managers had reached the same conclusion: All five change-management issues had relevance to the Starmark operations department and, by extension, to implementation of the just-in-time program. The strategic agenda had become clear. In directing the change, management would need to follow five strategies:

1. Reduce Uncertainty.
2. Secure a Commitment.
3. Issue a Challenge.
4. Forge a Single Agenda.
5. Implement Fairness.

SELECTING TACTICS... AND LAUNCHING THE PROGRAM

The production manager kept a list of change-management tactics that corresponded to the five strategies. He distributed a copy to each of his three colleagues. His instructions: Examine the list and identify which tactics will effectively promote the change.

"Before you start shaping the tactical agenda," the production manager noted, "determine what kinds of constraints we face. These can relate to time, personnel, organization—and perhaps other areas you may think of. On the time issue, well, we're not on a deadline. But we all know there's a lot of room for improvement. It would be nice to seize the benefits as soon as possible.

"With personnel, consider who'll be helping to implement the tactics. I'm heading up the program, but I certainly can't do everything. Consider the types of expertise that specific employees can bring to the project. I think it would be appropriate, for instance, for the inventory-control chief to be my main assistant on this project." He turned to the inventory manager. "After we get things in place, it'll be your baby."

After fielding several questions, the production manager continued:

"When you go through this list, remember to keep your mind open. Don't limit yourself to these tactics. You may think of other tactics associated with the five strategies that will work well in bringing JIT to Starmark."

One week passed while the four team members individually studied the tactics and made their selections. Then they gathered once again in the production manager's office. Comparing notes, they realized that the sheer breadth of the change prompted each of them to select nearly all the change tactics. What's more, several additional tactics not on the original list had been developed. "This is quite an undertaking, isn't it?" the production manager observed less than an hour into their meeting. His words echoed the thoughts of everyone in the room.

The meeting unfolded in an organized way. Each team member proposed a tactical agenda, explaining why the choices were made and how the tactics would promote the change. The production manager took notes, identifying common threads that linked each agenda and isolating areas in which someone offered a unique point of view. After all four presentations, the manager used his notes to lead the discussion. He took each strategy separately—beginning with "reduce uncertainty"—and summarized the tactics on which all team members agreed. Next, he noted where opinions differed. This led to an exchange in which team members explained the reasoning behind their positions. In some cases, the debate led to compromise. Other times, the discussion revealed errors in thinking. Slowly but steadily, the group began to develop a single tactical agenda.

The first day's meeting, which lasted a full four hours, covered only two change strategies. The next day, the team met again, this time for five hours. In the end, all four managers agreed on the set of tactics they would use to implement the JIT program. The tactics addressed all five issues that had a bearing on the Starmark operation: predictability, unity, pride, isolation, and fairness.

The team spent part of the next day developing an implementation schedule. The tactics formed an extensive agenda of managerial responsibilities, and it surprised no one that the schedule covered about a year. "Now, it's a matter of putting these tactics to work," the production manager said, concluding the meeting. "We've gone over what each of you will be doing during the implementation. Let's get things rolling."

A week later, things *were* rolling, pushed forward by a meeting with top management and orientation sessions with all employees. Meanwhile, the original team members kept an open ear directed to the plant floor to monitor response to the JIT launch. On several occasions, the production manager met separately with managers and employees who seemed overly skeptical. As the first week pushed into the second, third, and fourth, the production manager and his fellow change-managers:

Publicized top management's commitment to the JIT program. The president, joined by the operations VP and the production manager, declared his support during an all-operations meeting.

Launched training sessions, beginning with personnel who would be directly involved in JIT. Separately, each employee received an information packet that included facts about JIT and articles describing successful programs at other companies.

Set up a steering committee to deal with sensitive personnel issues. In the early weeks of the program, the committee began by setting its agenda. Responsibilities included: revising the performance-review process to address JIT, keeping employees updated on progress in implementing the new program, developing a special award to recognize outstanding performance, and so forth.

Began analyzing how JIT would affect other functional areas. The production manager planned to meet with managers from marketing, finance, accounting, and other departments to ensure they understood the implications of the changes underway in operations.

Developed a system for charting the progress of the implementation. The system would be important to motivate employees and create the sense that JIT was truly an employee program.

The above list is partial; even more tactics were put into action during the first month. Suffice to say that management—the entire operations department, for that matter—had its hands full. The coming months promised to be just as demanding.

If we were to fade out at this point and return to the scene a year later, what would we find? Would Starmark be enjoying reduced inventory costs, reduced setup times, and on-time deliveries? Would Starmark employees be won over by JIT, fully adopting the changes in their jobs? Would the future hold promise of continued acceptance and steady improvements to the bottom line?

The ongoing goal is to take steps to minimize the risk involved in any change effort—to stack the deck in favor of success. During our first two visits to Starmark, we saw a well-intentioned manager who left too much to chance. He started out determined to control the change process, but in the end, the process controlled him. The third time was different. The manager used a strategic change-management approach tailored to fit not only the type of change, but also Starmark's unique operations environment. The approach left nothing to chance.

Like the best of stories, this one ends happily. At last report, the JIT program is becoming a way of life at Starmark, and the benefits continue to unfold. The production manager remains firmly in control of the change process.

NOTES

CHAPTER 1
MANAGING CHANGE: AN OPERATIONS NECESSITY

1 Noel Tichy, "The Essentials of Strategic Change Management," *Journal of Business Strategy*, Spring 1983, p. 58.

2 Jacob M. Schlesinger, "GM to Retool Pittsburgh Stamping Plant to Parts Factory, Avoiding Closedown," *Wall Street Journal*, June 11, 1988, p. 18.

3 Kathleen Deveny, "For Caterpillar, the Metamorphosis Isn't Over," *Business Week*, Aug. 31, 1987, pp. 72-74.

4 Todd Vogel, "Big Changes are Galvanizing General Electric," *Business Week*, Dec. 15, 1989, pp. 100-102.

5 Bureau of the Census, Foreign Trade Division

6 Alan Murray, "The Service Sector's Productivity Problem," *Wall Street Journal*, Feb. 9, 1987, p. 1.

7 U.S. Bureau of Labor

8 Michael L. Tushman, William H. Newman, Elaine Romanelli, "Convergence and Upheaval: Managing the Unsteady Pace of Organizational Evolution," *California Management Review*, Fall 1986, p. 31.

9 David Wessel, "Service Industries Find Computers Don't Always Raise Productivity," *Wall Street Journal*, April 19, 1988, p. 37.

10 Kenneth Labich, "Big Changes at Big Brown," *Fortune*, Jan. 18, 1988, pp. 56-64.

11 Resa W. King, "UPS Gets a Big Package—of Computers," *Business Week*, July 25, 1988.

12 Wendy Zellner, "GM's New 'Teams' Aren't Hitting Any Homers," *Business Week*, August 8, 1988, pp. 46-47.

13 Ibid., p. 46.

CHAPTER 6
ISSUES, STRATEGIES, AND TACTICS

1 W. Brooke Tunstall, "The Breakup of the Bell System: A Case Study in Cultural Transformation," *California Management Review*, Winter 1986, pp. 110-124.

2 Daniel Quinn Mills, *Labor-Management Relations*, Third Edition (New York: McGraw-Hill, 1986), p. 62.

3 Michael Schuster, "Cooperation and Change in Union Settings: Problems and Opportunities," *Human Resource Management*, Summer 1984, p. 146.

4 Donald B. Thompson, "Rockwell's Bold New World," *Industry Week*, June 15, 1987, pp. 38-41.

5 Ibid., p. 41.

NOTES

NOTES

NOTES

NOTES

NOTES

NOTES

NOTES

NOTES

NOTES

NOTES

NOTES

ORDER FORM

1 -- SEND BOOK(S) TO:

NAME, TITLE: ______________________________

COMPANY: ______________________________

ADDRESS: ______________________________

____

PHONE: ________________________

2 -- ORDER:

PRICE PER BOOK:	$14.95	
QUANTITY DISCOUNT:	4-6 BOOKS 10%, 7+ BOOKS 20%	
SHIPPING COST:	First Book	Each Additional Book
	$2.50	50 cents

ORDER QUANTITY: ____________

PRICE PER BOOK: x $14.95

SUBTOTAL: ____________

QUANTITY DISCOUNT: – ____________

SUBTOTAL: ____________

5% SALES TAX: ____________
(N.C. sales only.)

SHIPPING COST: ____________

TOTAL: ____________

3 -- PAYMENT METHOD (check one):

_____ Check enclosed for full amount.

_____ Send an invoice for the full amount.
(Amount due within 30 days of delivery.)

P.O. number, if applicable: ____________

Direct invoice to: ____________________

____

4 -- SEND ORDER TO:

ARROW ASSOCIATES
P.O. BOX 470869
CHARLOTTE, N.C. 28247